# CAMPUS ARTIFACTS
## as Diversity Messages

A Photographic Approach

JAMES H. BANNING, PH.D.

TerraCotta
Publishing

# CAMPUS ARTIFACTS
## as Diversity Messages

James H. Banning© 2018

Email: campusecologist@gmail.com

Website: http://www.campusecologist.com

ISBN 13: 978-0-9977353-8-3

ISBN 10: 0-9977353-8-4


Library of Congress Control Number: 2018930315



Cover design and typesetting by Michelle Kenny, Windsor, CO

Printed in the United States of America


TerraCotta Publishing

Arvada, CO




TerraCotta
Publishing

# TABLE OF CONTENTS

Shade Boxes

# AN INTRODUCTORY NOTE

In 1984, J. B. Jackson, a pioneer landscape scholar, noted the following:

> Over and over again, I have said that the commonplace aspects
> of the contemporary landscape, the streets and houses and fields
> and places of work, could teach us a great deal not only about
> American history and American society, but about ourselves and
> how we relate to the world. It is a matter of learning how to see.

The purpose of this book reflects B. J. Jackson's statement: "learning
how to see" the college and university campus and to discover its
messages about diversity. Again, to use and transport Jackson's words
to the campus: The campus "is always open before us. We have but
to read it."

Jackson quotes from: Mendelsohn, J. & Wilson, C. (Eds.). (2015).
Drawn to landscape. Staunton, VA: George F. Thompson Publishing.

# PREFACE

The title of the book *Campus Artifacts as Diversity Messages: A Photographic Approach* sets the stage for its content. While there is a materiality to campus artifacts, they interface with campus constituents in interpretative ways to produce multiple meanings, and these artifacts can be photographed for discussions of campus culture—both the positive and negative aspects.

The material culture of the campus comprises the human-made objects that are viewable by the inhabitants of the campus, including those who are on campus for a substantial time—students, faculty, and staff—and the visitor who spends a shorter time. Many of these objects are intended and reflect considerable effort in design and implementation: the buildings, institutional artifacts, furniture arrangements, official signage, and the installation of various campus art forms—paintings, murals, and sculptures. Often, however, the material culture on display is not officially intended, designed, or approved, yet these items of material culture also send messages of culture; for example, graffiti, physical traces of behavior, and unofficial signage. In addition, even the objects intentionally designed for a specific message often take on meanings that were unintended.

The purpose of this book is a very practical one—to present a concise overview of ways to view the campus material environment (conceptual tools) and ways to interpret and understand the cultural messages embedded in the material culture (interpretative tools) using photographs to expose messages of diversity. The basic conceptual tools involve the concepts of the ecological perspective, material culture, and visual/photographic research. The interpretive tools are derived from the observational methods associated with environmental psychology and include an eclectic range of strategies primarily based in qualitative visual analysis.

This book takes the position that for a campus culture to be positive and healthy for its designed activities of education, research, and service, all inhabitants need to feel welcomed and not lost, safe and not endangered, and included rather than excluded. Given the changing nature of campus populations and the importance of social justice, the diversity messages associated with race, ethnicity, physical abilities, gender, sexual identities, and religion are ones that require institutional attention.

In chapter three, after presenting interpretive strategies and photographic illustrations of diversity messages, a taxonomy is presented to assist in attaching individual photographs to cultural themes. This chapter also presents ways to organize movement from reading and understanding of the campus material culture to intervention and implementation of change. Individual and group strategies are presented, highlighting the importance of campus participation and institutional feedback as a way for a campus to move toward a more welcoming, safe, and inclusive campus (Strange and Banning, 2015). A brief discussion is also presented on the removal of campus artifacts. The chapter closes with a discussion of ethical considerations important to photographing campus material culture.

**A final note:** Apologies to the reader and to "real" photographers for the quality of many of the photographs. They were taken during field activities where the focus was on capturing content for discussions.

# Reference:

Strange, C. C. & Banning, J. H. (2015). *Designing for learning: Creating campus environments for student success.* San Francisco, CA: Jossey-Bass.

# ACKNOWLEDGMENT

Sue Banning has given both personal and conceptual support to this project: always available to discuss ideas, edit my words, provide constructive feedback, and give the personal encouragement every writer needs.

In addition, I would like to thank all the campuses that have invited me to read and interpret their campus environments relating to diversity using photographs and to participate in their discussions aimed toward a more welcoming, safe, and inclusive campus. These institutions will not be named nor will photographs be associated with specific institutions. The photographs are very helpful in illustrating issues and giving practical examples for the concepts and tools of the book, but they represent only a "slice in time" for an institution. Many of the negative and troublesome campus photos have been addressed by the campuses; therefore, the photographs should be associated with the purpose of understanding the concepts and tools of the book and should not serve to embarrass a campus. Photographs in the book are used for illustration of concepts only and not to identify specific campuses.

Cover Note: Although the "Men Working" sign was found in front of a campus classroom building, the building in the cover photo is not that building. The lack of clarity in the original photo prohibited its use.

As always, there are many colleagues who have been persons of influence. On the topic of campus culture, I would like to acknowledge George Kuh, Elizabeth Whitt, and Carney Strange.

Thanks to Dr. Andrea Sims and TerraCotta Publishing for placing my thoughts in book form.

# LINES OF SCHOLARSHIP

### The Ecological Perspective, Material Culture, and Visual/Photographic Observations

During my supervision of doctoral dissertations, I often used a Western culture "social greeting" analogy to help students to sort out their review of literature efforts. Some literature finds should be treated like greeting an acquaintance from afar—you wave. Other literature should be treated like meeting a casual friend on the street—you say hello, shake hands, and have a short conversation. Finally, however you greet a very close friend—you hug! Literature finds should be treated in a similar manner: some you wave to, some you say hello to, and a few you will want to hug closely.

The intention of this book is to provide very practical ways to read and interpret the material culture of the campus setting. It is unwise to be practical, however, without at least noting some background scholarship for the practical efforts. Practice without theory is risky. The foundational scholarship topics include the ecological perspective, material culture, and visual/photographic research, and these topics will be viewed as scholarship "lines" (Ingold, 2015). There is not enough time and space in this book to give these topics a "hug," but they deserve more than a "wave." So, I will address each of the concepts with important literature citations and provide resource references and resource illustrations in sections noted as a shaded box. These efforts will serve as the "hello" and a door to the "hug." First, however, more about scholarship lines.

## Scholarship Lines

To organize the conceptual and literature background that supports the use of photographs to capture the messages of material culture, three conceptual/scholarship areas are important: an ecological perspective, understanding material culture, and visual/photographic research. I first thought of these three areas as the conceptual building blocks that support the purpose of this book, but after being exposed to the work of Ingold (2007, 2015, & 2016) and Hodder (2012) I think "lines" is a more useful terminology than "building blocks."

Ingold uses the concept of lines to explore anthropology and then suggests that the concept of lines promotes thinking about how lines become "entangled" together (Hodder, 2012) to form knots. These entangled lines eventually form surfaces that are referred to by Ingold (2015, p.83) as "meshwork." What I am suggesting is that we look at the lines of scholarship representing the ecological perspective, material culture, and visual/photographic research to form the entanglement or the surface for supporting the importance of understanding the cultural messages of a campus's material culture and capturing these messages in photographs. Of significance to campus life and the focus of this manuscript are the messages surrounding the notion of diversity.

These three lines of scholarship are not crisp sets or parallel lines but rather a fuzzy intersection. I first introduce the three lines of scholarship and then suggest in chapter two that Rapoport's (1982) nonverbal communication approach to material culture provides the "meshwork" for understanding how the ecological perspective, material culture, and visual/photographic research come together or "tangle" to give a practical approach to understanding campus culture. The notion of material culture playing a significant role in communicating culture is not new (Kuh, 1993; Kuh & Whitt, 1988; Whitt, 1993). Kuh and Whitt and their colleagues can provide an important "hug" for understanding campus culture.

**The Ecological Perspective Line**

As I noted in a recent publication (Banning, 2016), the ecological perspective's scholarship line is long and rich and impossible to cover in just a few pages. Etymology is a place to start. The word ecology stems from the Greeks and means the "study of the house" (Kormonday & Brown, 1998). Later, the word was involved in denoting the interaction of animals and their environment. Ecology was later in the mid-nineteenth century defined within the scientific community by Ernst Haeckel for use in the study of evolution (Kormonday & Brown, 1998). The next major movement was the establishment of the field of human ecology. It is the field of human ecology that serves as the immediate backdrop for the scholarship line for viewing the campus environment as an important issue to campus culture. Human ecology is defined as the study of the relationships between people and their environment (Marten, 2001). Campus ecology (Banning, 2016) takes the concept of human behavior in relation to the natural, social, and built environments and focuses on the college and university campus. For example, Banning and Kuk (2005) defined the concept of campus ecology as follows:

> The concept of campus ecology is defined as the study of the campus as an ecological system made up of three components. The first is the organism/inhabitant component which includes students, faculty, staff, visitors, and others associated with the campus. The second component is the settings/environments component, and it includes both the social environment (the curriculum, the co-curriculum, the extra-curricular, and other social functions) and the physical environment (buildings, landscapes, walkways, and other natural and constructed features of the environment). The third component is the activities/behaviors component (learning, research, personal development, and other outcomes specific to higher education). (p. 9)

In summary, the scholarship line of the ecological perspective underscores the importance of studying "campus as house" and the artifacts within that make up the material culture of the campus.

**Shade Box 1-1: Resource References for the Ecological Perspective**

Amedo, D., Golledge, R., & Stimson, R. (2009). *Person environment behavior research.* New York: The Guildford Press.

Banning, J. H. (Ed.). (1978). *Campus ecology: A perspective for student affairs.* Cincinnati, OH: NASPA Monograph.

Banning, J. H. (2016). *Campus ecology and university affairs: History, Applications, and Future.* Arvada, CO: TerraCotta Publishing.

Banning, J. H.,& Kaiser, L. (1974). Ecological perspective and model for campus design. *The Personnel and Guidance Journal, 52*(6), 370-375.

Barker, R. G. (1968*). Ecological psychology: Concepts and methods for studying the environment of human behavior.* Stanford, CA: Stanford University Press.

Bronfenbrenner, U. (1979). *The ecology of human development: Experiments by nature and  design.* Cambridge, MA: Harvard University Press.

Brunswik, E. (1956). *Perception and the representative design of psychological experiments.* Berkeley, CA: University of California Press.

Conyne, R. K., & Clack, R. J. (1981). *Environmental assessment and design.* New York: Praeger Publishers.

Heft, H. (2001). *Ecological psychology in context.* New York: Psychology Press.

Kelly, J. G. (2006). *Becoming ecological: An expedition into community psychology.* New York: Oxford University Press.

Kemp, S., Whittaker, J., & Tracy, E. (1997). *Person-environment practice: The social ecology of interpersonal helping.* New York: Adline De Gruyter.

Kormonday, E. J., & Brown, D. E. (1998). *Fundamentals of Human Ecology.* Upper Saddle River, NJ: Prentice-Hall.

Lewin, K. (1936). *Principles of topological psychology.* New York: McGraw Hill.

Michael, W. B., & Boyer, E. L. (1965). Campus environment. *Review of Educational Research, 35*(4), 264-276.

Stern, G. G. (1965). Student ecology and the college environment. *Journal of Medical Education, 40,* 132-54.

Strange, C. C., & Banning, J. H. (2001). *Educating by design: Creating campus environments That work.* San Francisco, CA: Jossey-Bass.

Strange, C. C., & Banning, J. H. (2015). *Designing for learning: Creating campus environments for student success.* San Francisco, CA: Jossey-Bass.

Walsh, W. B. (1973). Theories of person-environment interaction: Implications for the college student. Iowa City, IA: American College Testing Program.

Walsh, W. B. (1978). Person/Environment Interaction. In. J. H. Banning (Ed). *Campus ecology: A Perspective for Student Affairs* (pp. 6-16). Cincinnati, OH: National Student Personnel.

## The Material Culture Line

The concept of material culture falls within several disciplines, and its definition has loose boundaries. Berger (2014) refers to material culture as the "world of things that people make" (p. 16). "Stuff" is the concept used by Miller (2010, p. 1). For the purposes of this manuscript, Prown's (1982) definition is helpful: "The term *material culture* ... refers quite directly and efficiently, if not elegantly, both to the subject matter of the study, *material*, and to its purpose, the understanding of *culture*" (p. 2). Berger (2014) best describes and summarizes the scholarship line of material culture:

> Cultural values and beliefs take form or are manifested in artifacts and objects—that is, in material culture. What this suggests is that we can use artifacts to help us gain insights into the culture that produced them, if we know how to interpret or "read" them. Material culture gives us a means of understanding better the societies and cultures that produce the objects and use them." (p. 17)

The material culture line of scholarship provides the conceptual support to the key notion of this manuscript that campus artifacts contain messages (encoded) by the campus culture and that these messages can be read (decoded) by inhabitants and visitors to the campus. Campus messages regarding diversity are a prime example of this encoding and decoding process. The purpose of this book is further supported by Berger (2014) when he notes: "Generally speaking, we can say that if you can photograph it and it isn't too large, we can consider it to be an example of material culture" (p. 17). The next section of this introductory chapter presents the third scholarship line: Visual/Photographic Research.

**Shade Box 1-2: Resource References for Material Culture**

Berger, A. (2014). *What objects mean: An introduction to material culture.* (2nd Edition). Walnut Creek, CA: Left Costal Press.

Csikszentmihalyi, M., & Rochberg-Halton, E. (1981). *The meaning of things: Domestic symbols and the self.* Cambridge, UK: Cambridge University Press.

Deely, J. (1982). *Introducing semiotics: Its history and doctrine.* Bloomington: Indiana University Press.

Frutiger, A. (1989). *Signs and symbols.* New York: Van Nostrand Reinhold.

Geertz, C. (1973). *The interpretation of cultures*. New York: Basic Books.

Hodder, I. (2012). *Entangled: An Archaeology of the relationships between humans and things*. West Sussex, UK: Wiley-Blackwell Publishers.

Hodge, R., & Kress, G. (1988). *Social semiotics*. Ithaca, NY: Cornell University Press.

Ingold, T. (2015). *The life of lines*. London: Routledge Classics.

Ingold, T. (2016). *Lines*. New York: Routledge Classics.

Lubar, S., & Kingery, W. D. (1993). *History of things: Essays on material culture*. Washington, D.C.: Smithsonian Institution.

Miller, D. (2010). *Stuff*. Malden, MA: Polity.

Money, A. (2007). *Material culture and the living room. Journal of Consumer Culture, 7*(3), 355-377.

Myers, F. R. (2002). *The empire of things: Regimes of value and material culture*. Santa Fe, NM: School of American Research Press.

Prown, J. D. (1982). Mind in matter: An introduction to material culture theory and method. *Winterthur Portfolio, 17*(1), 1-19.

Sebeok, T. (1986). (Ed.) *Encyclopedia dictionary of semiotics*. New York: Mouton de Gruyter.

Sless, D. (1986). *In search of semiotics*. Totowa, NJ: Barnes and Nobel Books.

Tilley, C. (1999). *Metaphor and material culture*. Oxford, UK: Blackwell Publishers.

Tilley, C., Keane, W., Kuchler, S., Rowlands, M., & Spyer, P. (Eds.). (2006). *Handbook of material culture*. London: Sage Publications.

## Architectural Readings

Bonta, J. (1979). *Architecture and its interpretation: A study of expressive systems in architecture.* London: Lund Humphries.

Preziosi, D. (1979). *The semiotics of the built environment: An introduction to architectonic analysis.* Bloomington: Indiana University Press.

Rapoport, A. (1982). *The meaning of the built environment.* Beverly Hills, CA: Sage Publications.

Clarke, D. S. (1987). *Principles of semiotics.* New York: Routledge & Kegan.

### Visual/Photographic Research Line

Observational methods fall into two categories: obtrusive and unobtrusive (Webb, Campbell, Schwartz, & Sechrest, 1996). The obtrusive methods involve the observer being placed directly into the phenomena of interest and the presence of the observer influencing the observation. Unobtrusive methods gather observational data but without direct involvement with the people of interest. The unobtrusive is also referred to as non-reactive observation (Lee, 2000). An example important to this manuscript is the use of photographs (Emmison & Smith, 2000) to capture the meaning of campus cultural artifacts. This method places emphasis on the visual rather than the verbal.

Sanoff (1991) stated that much of historical environmental research has "relied on verbal descriptions and perceptions of the physical environment, virtually ignoring the importance of the visual component" (p. ix). Willig (2011) makes a similar observation: "(There is a) ... noticeable lack of accommodation of the 'visual' in contemporary qualitative psychology ... (it can) enrich our understanding of meaning-making and experience ... can add to our understanding of the human experience" (p.xxv). Rose (2007) notes the importance of the visual image in understanding "how social life happens" (p. xii). Reavey (2011) underlines cultural connection to the visual by noting that the "visual is an integral part of the way in which culture operates (p. xxvi). The connection of the visual to the cultural is similarly endorsed by Prosser (1998), when he states that the visual is a "significant manifestation of culture" (p. 2). The advantages of the visual approach are outlined by Spencer (2011). He notes that the visual is immediate and explicit, that it can help to create narratives, and that it provides "a 'thick description' that helps in exploring and finding meaning" (p. 33).

Key to this supporting line of visual scholarship is the link between the visual as observation to using photographs to capture the meaning of the visual. Raggel and Shratz (2004) pointing to the visual and the use of photographs state: "… (photographs) demonstrated how social life is frequently situated, shaped, and given social significance by the interaction of individuals, with artifacts and spaces" (p. 7). As will be highlighted in chapter two of this manuscript, the link between artifacts in the campus environment and the interpretation of photographs of those artifacts is complex. The adage that "pictures don't lie" fails to capture the complexity of the interpretative process going from the photograph to its meaning, even the complexity of which artifacts are chosen to be photographed. Ball (1998) makes this point very clear: "As a form of data, photographs are not capable of talking for themselves, the information has to be teased out of them, interpreted and decoded, the visual availability of the phenomena has to be unpacked" (p. 137). Byers (1966) gives a succinct summary: "cameras don't take pictures, people do" (p. 27). My role as the photographer/interpreter regarding diversity will be addressed in chapter three.

### Shade Box 1-3: Resource References for Visual/Photographic Research

#### Visual References: General

Ball, M. S., & Smith, G. W. H. (1992). *Analyzing visual data* (Qualitative Research Methods Series, Vol. 24). Newbury Park, CA Sage.

Banks, M. (2007). *Using visual data in qualitative research.* Los Angeles: Sage Publication.

Banks, M., & Morphy, H. (Eds.). (1997). *Rethinking visual anthropology.* New Haven, CT: Yale University Press.

Barthes, R. (1996). *Camera Lucida: Reflections on Photography.* New York: Hill and Wang.

Bauer, M. W. & Gaskell, G. (Eds.) (2000). *Qualitative researching with text, image, and sound.* London: Sage.

Becker, H. S. (1978). Do photographs tell the truth? *After Image, 5,* 9-13.

Becker, H. S. (1986). *Doing things together: Selected papers.* Evanston, IL: Northwestern Press.

Collier, J. J., & Collier, M. (1986). *Visual anthropology: Photography as a research method.* Albuquerque, NM: University of New Mexico Press.

Dabbs, J. M. (1982). Making things visible. In J. Van Maanen, J. M. Dabbs, & R. Faulkner, (Eds.). *Varieties of Qualitative Research* (pp. 31-64). London: Sage.

Denzin, N. K. (1989). *The research act* (3rd ed.) Englewood Cliffs, NJ: Prentice-Hall.

Emmison, M., & Smith, P. (2000). *Researching the visual.* London: Sage Publications.

Graeme, S. (2005). *Art practice as research. Inquiry in the visual arts.* Thousand Oaks, CA: Sage.

Harper, D. (1989). Visual Sociology: Expanding sociological vision. In G. Bank, J. L. McCartney and E. Brent. (Eds.). *New Technologies in sociology: Practical application in research and work* (pp. 81-97). New Brunswick, NJ: Transaction Books.

Harper, D. (1994). On the authority of the image: Visual Methods at the crossroads. In N. Denzin, & Y. S. Lincoln, (Eds.). *Handbook of Qualitative Research* (pp.403-12). London, Sage.

Hesse-Biber, S. N., & Leavy, P. (Eds.). (2008). *Handbook of emergent methods.* New York: Guilford Press.

Hockings, P. (Ed.) (1995). *Principles of visual anthropology.* (2nd Edition) Berlin: Mouton de        Gruyter.

Knowles, J. G., & Cole, A. L. (Eds.). (2008). *Handbook of the arts in qualitative research.* Los Angeles: Sage.

Pink, S. (2001). *Doing visual ethnography.* London: Sage Publications.

Pole, C. (Ed.). (2004). *Seeing is believing? Approaches to visual research.* London: Elsevier.

Prosser, J. (Ed.). (1998). *Image-based research: A sourcebook for qualitative researchers.* London: Falmer Press.

Rose, G. (2007). *Visual methodologies: An introduction to the interpretation of visual materials.* (2nd ed.). Los Angeles: Sage Publications.

Smith, K., Moriarty, S., Barbatsis, G., & Kenney, K. (Eds). (2005*). Handbook of visual communication: Theory, methods, and media.* Mahwah, NJ: Lawrence Erlbaum Assoc. Publishers.

Stanczak, G. C. (Ed.). (2007). *Visual research methods: Image, society, and representation.* Los Angeles: Sage.

Sturken, M., & Cartwright, L. (2001). *Practice of looking: An introduction to visual culture.* Oxford, NY: Oxford Press.

Templin, P. A. (1982). Still photography in evaluation. In N. L. Smith (Ed.). *Communication strategies in evaluation.* (pp. 121-175). Beverly Hills, CA: Sage.

Thomson, P. (Ed). (2008). *Doing visual research with children and young people*. London: Routledge.

Van Leeuwen, T., & Jewitt, C. (2001). *Handbook of visual analysis*. London: Sage Publications.

Wagner, J. (Ed.). (1979). *Images of information*. Beverly Hills, CA: Sage.

Wang, C., & Burris, M. A. (1997). Photovoice: Concept, methodology, and use for participatory needs assessment. *Health education & behavior, 24*(3), 369-387.

Wang, C. C., Yi, W. K., Tao, Z. W., & Carovano, K. (1998). Photovoice as a participatory health promotion strategy. *Health promotion international, 13*(1), 75-86.

### Visual References: Personal/Applied Work

Banning, J. H. (1992). Visual anthropology: Viewing the campus ecology for messages of sexism. *The Campus Ecologist, 10*(1), 1-4.

Banning, J. H. (1995). Campus images: Homoprejudice. *The Campus Ecologist, 12*(3), 3.

Banning, J. H. (1997). Assessing the Campus' Ethical Climate: A Multidimensional approach. In J. Fried, (Ed). *Ethics for today's Campus: New Perspectives on education, student development, and institutional management* (pp. 95-105). (New Direction for Student Services #77), San Francisco: Jossey-Bass Publishers.

Banning, J. H., & Bartels, S. (1997). A taxonomy: Campus physical artifacts as communicators of Campus multiculturalism. *NASPA Journal, 35*(1), 29-37.

Banning, J. H., & McKelfresh, D. A. (1998). Using photographs of the housing mission statement in staff training. *Talking Stick, 15*(8), 22-24.

Banning, J. H., Middleton, V., & Deniston, T. L. (2008). Using photographs to assess equity climate: A taxonomy. *Multicultural Perspectives, 10*(1), 41-46.

Banning, J. H., & Luna, F. C. (1992). Viewing the campus ecology for messages about Hispanic/Latino culture. *The Campus Ecologist 10* (4), 1-4.

Banning, J. H., Sexton, J., Most, D. E. & Maier, S. (2007). Gender asymmetries encountered in the search and exploration of mining engineering program websites: A portrayal of posture and roles. *Journal of Women and Minorities in Science and Engineering 13*, 165-176.

Kaminski, K., & Banning, J. (2007) Visuals in public places: Whose interpretation is it? In R. E. Griffin, M. D. Averinou, & J. Gieson (Eds.). *History, community, and culture: Celebrating tradition and transforming the future* (pp.109-114). Indianapolis, IN: IDEC.

Marley, J., Nobe, M. C., Clevenger, C. M. & Banning, J. H. (2015). Participatory post-occupancy evaluation (PPOE): A method to include students in evaluating health-promoting attributes of a green school. *Children, Youth, and Environments, 25*(1), 4-28.

Sexton, J. M., O'Connell, S., Banning, J. H., & Most, D. (2014). Characteristics and culture of geoscience departments as interpreted from their website photographs. *Journal of Women and Minorities in Science and Engineering, 20*(93), 257-278.

The Campus Ecologist articles are available at http://www.campusecologist.com

## Summary

In summary, the ecological perspective highlights the focus on the environment as a significant factor in determining behavior and examining culture. Within the environment resides the material culture of the built environment and adornments that provide opportunity for photographing and interpreting the cultural messages. The elements/objects of the material culture can be observed and photographed for discussion and evaluation, and, if needed, they can be changed.

In chapter two, I introduce Rapoport's (1982) nonverbal communication approach to material culture as providing the "meshwork" for understanding how the ecological perspective, material culture, and visual/photographic research come together in a "tangle" or "knot" to give a practical approach to understanding campus culture.

# References:

Ball, M. (1998). Remarks on visual competence as an integral part of ethnographic fieldwork practice: The visual availability of culture. In J. Prosser, (Ed.). *Image-based research: A sourcebook for qualitative researchers* (pp.131-147). London: Falmer Press.

Banning, J. H. (2016). *Campus ecology and university affairs: History, applications, and future.* Arvada, CO: TerraCotta Publishing.

Banning, J. H., & Kuk, L. (2005). Campus ecology and college student health. *Spectrum,* November 9-15.

Berger, A. (2014). *What objects mean: An introduction to material culture.* (2nd Edition). Walnut Creek, CA: Left Costal Press.

Byers, P. (1966). "Cameras don't take pictures." *Columbia University Forum, 9,* 27-31. Emmison, M., & Smith, P. (2000). *Researching the visual.* London: Sage Publications.

Hodder, I. (2012). *Entangled: An Archaeology of the relationships between humans and things.* West Sussex, UK: Wiley-Blackwell Publishers.

Ingold, T. (2007). *Lines: A brief history.* Abingdon, UK: Routledge.

Ingold, T. (2015). *The life of lines.* London: Routledge Classics.

Ingold, T. (2016). *Lines.* New York: Routledge Classics.

Kormonday, E. J., & Brown, D. E. (1998). *Fundamentals of Human Ecology.* Upper SaddleRiver, NJ: Prentice-Hall.

Kuh, G. D. (Ed.). (1993). *Cultural perspectives in student affairs work.* Washington, D.C. American College PersonnelAssociation.

Kuh, G. D., & Whitt, E. J. (1988). The invisible tapestry: Cultures in American colleges and universities. ASHE-ERIC Higher Education Report, No. 1. Washington, C. Association for the Study of Higher Education.

Lee, R. M. (2000). *Unobtrusive methods in social research.* Buckingham, UK: Open University Press.

Marten, G. G. (2001). *Human ecology: Basic concepts for sustainable development.* Sterling, VA: Earthscan Publications Ltd.

Miller, D. (2010). *Stuff.* Cambridge, UK: Polity Press.

Prosser, J. (Ed.). (1988). Introduction. In J. Prosser, (Ed.). *Image-based research: A sourcebook for qualitative researchers* (pp. 1-5). London: Falmer Press.

Prown, J. D. (1982). Mind in matter: An introduction to material culture theory and method. *Winterthur Portfolio, 17*(1), 1-19.

Raggel, A., & Shratz, M. (2004). Using visuals to release pupil's voices: Emotional pathways into enhancing thinking and reflecting on learning. In C. Pole (Ed.). *Seeing is believing? Approaches to visual research* (pp. 147-181). Amsterdam, NL: Elsevier.

Rapoport, A. (1982). *The meaning of the built environment: A nonverbal communications approach.* Beverly Hills, CA: Sage Publications.

Reavey, P. (Ed.) (2011). *Visual methods in psychology: Using and interpreting images in qualitative research.* New York: Psychology Press.

Rose, G. (2007). *Visual methodologies: An introduction to the interpretation of visual materials.* (2nd ed.). Los Angeles: Sage Publications.

Spencer, S. (2011). *Visual research methods in the social sciences: Awakening visions.* London: Routledge.

Sanoff, H. (1991). *Visual research methods in design.* New York: Van Nostrand Reinhold.

Webb, E. J., Campbell, D. T., Schwartz, R. D., & Sechrest. L. (1996). *Unobtrusive measures: Nonreactive research in the social sciences.* Chicago, IL: Rand McNally.

Whitt, E. J. (1993). Making the familiar strange: Discovering culture. In G. D. Kuh (Ed.). *Cultural perspectives in student affairs work* (pp.81-94). Washington, D.C. American College PersonnelAssociation.

Willig, C. (2011). Forward. In P. Reavey (Ed.) *Visual methods in psychology: Using and interpreting images inqualitative research.* (p. xxv). New York: Psychology Press.

# 2

# VISUAL/PHOTOGRAPHIC INTERPRETATIVE TOOLS

Chapter one established the importance of both the campus environment and the messages of material culture and that these environmental/cultural messages can be observed and photographed. This chapter introduces the concept of nonverbal communication as the mechanism of communication associated with material culture and the tools for how to read/interpret these messages.

## Rapoport's Non-Verbal Approach: Knitting the Lines of Scholarship

The link between the material culture and campus behavior involves the mechanism of non-verbal communication (Rapoport, 1982). He notes: "Since environments apparently provide cues for behavior, but do not do it verbally, it follows that they must represent a form of nonverbal behavior" (p. 50). Rapoport goes on to summarize: "… environments are more than just inhibiting, facilitating, or even catalytic, they not only remind, they also predict and describe" (p. 77). The material culture of the campus communicates to the campus inhabitants via non-verbal communication both the description of and the prescription of culture. In other words, institutional values, beliefs, and "how things are done around here," are communicated by the campus artifacts. The building designs and architecture, art, sculpture, posters, signs, and graffiti all contribute to the telling and reminding of the campus culture. The reminding function of the material culture or its mnemonic function is illustrated in Shade Box 2-1.

Again, to quote Rapoport: "The mnemonic function of the environment … reminding people of the behavior expected of them

... takes the remembering from the person and places the reminding in the environment" (p. 80–81). In other words, the material culture contains the encoded information, and the campus inhabitant decodes the cultural information by the mechanism of non-verbal communication. The material culture teaches; and by the processes of observing and interpreting, the teaching lessons can be deciphered or decoded, and—to underscore the thesis of this book—they can be photographed!

## Shade Box 2-1: Illustration of the Rapoport's Mnemonic Function

### The Built Environment: Do Ivy Walls Have Memories?

Perhaps a strange question. Certainly, walls do not contain memory cells. Literally, there are no "memory storage units" imbedded in the structures of the built environment on college campuses, but the structure and settings of our built environment do appear to "remind" us of certain behaviors. Amos Rapoport (1982) refers to this "reminding" as the mnemonic function of the environment. The environment thus communicates, through a whole set of cues, the most appropriate choices to be made: the cues are meant to elicit appropriate emotions, interpretations, behaviors, and transactions by setting up the appropriate situations and contexts.

"The environment can thus be said to act as a mnemonic ... It takes the remembering from the person and places the reminding in the environment" Rapoport (1982, pp. 80–81). The built environments on our campuses were constructed with encoded messages. When they are decoded through student behavior, a reminding or mnemonic function has occurred. By analyzing the built environments, a more complete understanding can be provided of the student behavior that occurs in these settings as well as a greater understanding of the contribution that environments make to student behavior. In fact, an analysis of the "reminding" given by built environments often produces a different and useful perspective. For example, the growing problem of "rowdy student behavior" at commencement ceremonies can be studied by such an analysis.

## Student Commencement Behavior

Over the past few years, there has been an increasing concern expressed by the faculty and administration over the ever-increasing incidents of inappropriate behavior at commencement ceremonies. It is common to hear graduation referred to as the "college circus." Recently, one institution asked a faculty committee to review the deterioration of student commencement behavior and to make recommendations for improvement. During one of the work sessions, one faculty member asked an interesting question. He wondered how each new graduating class could pick up on the previous student commencement behavior, since few undergraduates ever attended a graduation prior to their own. The answer to this question, in part, is that the cues for the inappropriate behavior are in the built environment. The setting "reminds" the student of certain behavior.

## It works this way!

The commencement exercises for this particular institution (as for most others) are held in the basketball field house. Students are seated by colleges on foldout bleachers next to the court floor. (Same seating as at basketball games.) The physical setting (backboards and scoreboards are still visible), and the seating arrangement cues "sporting behavior" not "graduation behavior." In fact, at one recent commencement ceremony, the students on the south side of the court yelled to their counterparts sitting on the north side: "We've got spirit, how about you?" The students on the north replied in a louder voice: "We've got spirit, HOW ABOUT YOU?" This back and forth volley continued with ever increasing volume for several minutes.

The above behavior is appropriate for a sporting event, but not for commencement exercises. However, the encoded messages of the built environment" remind students of the yelling and cheering associated with competitive sporting events. In fact, by arranging students by colleges, each with their own banner, "competitive teams" are formed to enhance the rowdiness called for by the field house environment. Institutions that are small enough to still hold commencement in the college chapel probably do not have the severe rowdy behavior problem. The encoded messages in that setting elicit behavior more compatible to the behavior that faculty and administrators are seeking for graduation ceremonies.

### Intervention Strategy

By taking into account the mnemonic function, the faculty committee recommended that students should not be seated in the bleachers but that chairs be placed on the floor. Such an arrangement should cue behaviors that are more "church or meeting" like in nature rather than the "sporting event" behavior. Obviously, many other factors go into student commencement behavior than just the physical setting and the seating arrangement. However, these built environmental factors may be far more important than previously thought.

### Ivy Walls: A Final Thought

Bloom (1977) suggests that the upper limit on the ability to predict human behavior solely on the basis of personal characteristics is relatively low. He further suggests that person-only conceptualizations leave perhaps three-quarters of the variation in human behavior unexplained. How much of the variation can be explained by the mnemonic function of the built environment? Perhaps in the future, counselors and student-personnel workers will be replaced by architects and carpenters! Probably not, but the possibility has some merit!

Are we not, now, attending to the many problems produced by earlier architects and carpenters?

**References:**

Bloom, B. L. (1977). *Community Mental Health*. Monterey, CA: Brooks/Cole Publishing Company.

Rapoport, A. (1982). *The Meaning of the Built Environment: A Nonverbal Communication Approach*. Beverly Hills, CA: Sage Publications.

## The Interpretations of Photographs

Why take photographs? There can be many answers to this question, but for the efforts represented in this book, you take photographs to assist the campus in understanding itself and, depending on the resulting understanding, to find ways to improve and enhance the positive and ways to address the negative messages. Visual images are critical to the process of understanding campus culture, but visual images need interpretation. If non-verbal communication is the voice of cultural artifacts, then the interplay of artifact characteristics and the life experiences of the interpreter becomes a critical factor in understanding the potential messages of the artifacts. The messages are not "fixed" by the material object itself but can vary depending upon the observer's background and their interpretative process. Kaminski and Banning (2007) noted this relationship:

> When an individual views a visual representation, be it a piece of art such as a statue, a poster on the wall, or a design of a building, their beliefs, values, and needs are factors that determine how the message is comprehended. (p. 109)

Different viewers can have different interpretations. The decoding process includes both the artifact and its encoded messages and the values and life experiences of the observer/photographer. Rather than seeing the multiple interpretations as a "threat to validity" of the messages, I take a more postmodern stance and see the multiple interpretations contributing to a richer discussion of the meaning of the artifact.

## Tools for Interpretation of Photographs: An Eclectic Approach

The next sections of this chapter provide tools for understanding an eclectic and practical approach to interpreting the campus photographs of campus material culture. This eclectic approach is built around the process of asking questions of the material culture of interest. Answers to the following questions help in providing the information needed for forming the interpretation of the artifact message. These questions can be viewed in a postmodern perspective as tools for deconstruction of the images. The interpretative frame is designed around asking the following questions.

### Basic Question: Manifest or Latent?

First, there is the basic question of whether the message of the artifact is manifest or latent (Neuendorf, 2000). If manifest, then few interpretive questions need to be asked; the message is self-evident and obvious. It is the denotation of the image, but if the message is more latent or hidden, then additional questions are needed to help the interpretation. Kaminski and Banning (2007) state: "The latent content is covert, it is the connotation of the image, and interpretative strategies come into play" (p. 109). The more the images fall in the direction of latent/conative, the greater the need for interpretive skills. While the concepts manifest and latent and others that follow are presented as dichotomies/binaries, they should be treated as "fuzzy" and not "crisp" (Ragin, 2008). There is considerable overlap between and among the question categories, and multiple questions are often needed to form the interpretation of the image.

### Additional Questions: Tools for Deconstruction

*Does the photograph of the cultural artifact contain binary oppositions?*

Look for arrangement of elements in pairs (Emmison & Smith, 2000). For example, male versus female, old versus young, and a myriad of other possibilities exist. The following are questions stemming from the binary perspective that I have found particularly useful in my interpretative process.

*What is the relationship among the elements in the photograph in terms of foreground and background?*

The more "important" elements of the photograph appear as the foreground. For example, in many photographs of poster materials, men appear in the foreground and women in the background. If the photo includes more than one race or ethnicity, then often the White figures are in the foreground and persons of color are in the background. If multiple roles are depicted in the photograph, then you often find the most important role in the foreground and less important roles in the background. A related tool is the concept of *juxtaposition*. How are the items in the photo positioned to each other?

*What is the relationship among the people in the photograph in terms of body position?*

Messages of power in photographs are communicated by body position (Branaman, 2001; Emmison & Smith, 2000). Typically, the person standing is associated with more power than those sitting (Banning, Sexton, Most, & Maier, 2007). For example, photographs of office settings often show the male figure standing over the female working at a desk. Teachers are most often seen as standing in a classroom while students are seated.

*What is the relationship among the overt public messages given via institutional publications like institutional advertisements, mission statements, recruitment materials, etc., and the messages found in the campus cultural artifacts?*

Many campuses use photographs of groups of students engaged in a variety of activities that include a diverse student group—for example, academic field trips. However, if you go to the academic departments, they often have posted their activities like field trips, etc., but seldom do you find the mix of students like those in the university's recruitment material. Universities often promote themes in their publications—for example, women in science. Again, if you go to the science departments on campus, you do not find the theme being portrayed in local artifacts (posters, activity photographs, departmental rosters). The binary of what is being written by the university and what is being done "on the ground" is clearly present.

*What roles are depicted in the artifact photograph, and to which person characteristics are they assigned? What roles are missing for specific groups?*

From my experience, nearly every K–12 poster I have photographed that has an African American student shows that student holding a basketball, suggesting the only path forward for Black students is athletics. Science roles are often represented by males only. In other words, many photographs of cultural artifacts carry the messages of vocational stereotyping.

*What symbols and associated meanings are included in the artifact photograph?*

The artifacts of campus material culture send symbolic messages (Gagliardi, 1990). Pillars/columns can suggest the cultural message of strength. These are most often found as part of the architectural structure of administration buildings. Restroom symbols suggest the campus's position regarding many gender issues. These are just a couple of examples, but there are a myriad of possibilities on campus.

*Does the artifact photograph suggest a narrative?*

Does the photograph (or many times the series of photographs) tell a story? Is there a story line (Emmison and Smith, 2000)? Often, an academic department will have a series of murals depicting the history of their discipline. Within the series, there are stories imbedded regarding gender and race. The role of women can often be found in the "series of leadership" photographs posted on the walls of the administration building. Do women appear in the series of leadership photographs? When do they appear? What is their role?

These observations can lead to the narrative or story of institutional female leadership.

*Do the elements of the "Behavioral/Physical Traces" observational method (Zeisel, 1975, 1981, 2006) help in the interpretation of the cultural artifact?*

The behavioral trace method is built on the notion that as we use cultural artifacts in our environment, traces of that use or behavior can be detected. These behavioral traces can be interpreted as non-verbal messages that increase the understanding of campus behavior and can be photographed (Banning, 1988). Zeisel's work focuses on four types of behavioral/physical trace categories. The *by-product of use* category includes the messages of erosion, leftovers, missing traces, and accretions. The category of *adaptation of use* captures how the artifacts of the campus are moved, connected, and separated by behavioral use. The third category is *displays of self*, which captures how we use the physical artifacts in the processes of personalization and identification and in communicating group membership. Finally, the last category is *public messages*. Three types of messages are described: official, unofficial, and illegitimate. (See Appendix A for a full description of Zeisel's observational method with examples and photo illustrations.)

**Summary**

The visual research opens the door to an important path to understanding campus culture. The messages of the buildings, art, symbols and signs, and other components of the campus material culture can be captured by photographs allowing for the use of interpretative tools to tease out possible important cultural meanings. Chapter three will include illustrations of these interpretative tools focusing on diversity. With the illustrations will be my interpretations—unavoidable, given the interpretative process discussed in this chapter.

## References:

Banning, J. H. (1988) Behavioral traces: A concept for campus ecologists. *The Campus Ecologist, 6*(2), 1,3.

Banning, J. H., Sexton, J., Most, D. E., & Maier, S. (2007). Gender asymmetries encountered in the search and exploration of mining engineering program web sites: A portrayal of posture and roles. *Journal of Women and Minorities in Science and Engineering, 13* (2), 165-174.

Branaman, A. (Ed.). (2001). *Self and society.* New York: Blackwell Publishers.

Emmison, M. & Smith, P. (2000). *Researching the visual.* London: Sage Publications.

Gagliardi, P. (Ed.). (1990). *Symbols and artifacts: Views of the corporate landscape.* New York: Aldine de Gruyter.

Kaminski, K. & Banning, J. H. (2007). Visuals in public places: Whose interpretation is it? In R. E. Griffin, M. D. Averinou, & J. Gieson (Eds). *History, community and culture: Celebrating tradition and transforming the future* (pp. 109-114). Madison, WI: IDEC.

Neuendorf, K. A. (2000). *The content analysis guidebook.* Thousand Oaks: CA: Sage Publications.

Ragin, C. C. (2008). *Redesigning social inquiry: Fuzzy sets and beyond.* Chicago, IL: Chicago University Press.

Rapoport, A. (1982). *The meaning of the built environment: A nonverbal communications approach.* Beverly Hills, CA: Sage Publications.

Zeisel, J. (1975). *Sociology and architectural design.* New York: Russell Sage Foundation.

Zeisel, J. (1981). *Inquiry by design.* Monterey, CA: Brooks/Cole.

Zeisel, J. (2006). *Inquiry by design: Environment/behavior/ neuroscience in architecture, interiors, landscape, and planning.* New York: W. W. Norton & Company.

# PHOTOGRAPHING CAMPUS DIVERSITY MESSAGES

### What I bring to the interpretative process

Illustrations of interpreting campus artifacts focusing on diversity follow in this chapter. Ideology not only influences the interpretation of images, as noted in chapter two, but it also guides the camera. The camera does not take pictures, the photographers do—they choose what to photograph, suggesting they have an interpretation of why the photo is important. Given the importance of what the observer brings to the interpretative process, I have provided a brief overview of what I bring to the observation/interpretative process regarding diversity (see Shade Box 3-1). Chapter three includes illustrations of the interpretative tools focusing on diversity from chapter two. Alongside the illustrations are my interpretations—unavoidable given the interpretative process. It is incumbent that I make known what I bring to the observing, photographing, and interpretative process of finding meaning in the material culture relating to diversity. Shade Box 3-1 presents a summary of my thoughts that I bring to the interpretative process regarding campus diversity.

### Shade Box 3-1: My Interpretative Stance on Diversity

Diversity has many meanings. The following definition by Winkle-Wagner and Locks (2017) captures the foundation of how it is used within this manuscript and my interpretive stance:

"... we focus particularly on diversity as it relates to those students who have historically been excluded, marginalized, or disallowed from participation in postsecondary institutions because of their racial or ethnic background" (p. xii).

To this foundation of exclusion, marginalization, and disallowed participation, issues related to gender, sexual orientation, disabilities, and religion are also included in my use of the concept of diversity. The importance of engaging all students with full participation within the institutional fabric is of critical importance to student success (Quaye & Harper, 2015).

### Important Conceptual Frameworks

There are several important conceptual frameworks and related scholarship that help shape and guide my thinking about diversity: Nancy Fraser's framework of redistribution, recognition, affirmation, and transformation relating to "parity of participation" (2003); James Banks's (2003) framework for understanding approaches to multicultural education and curriculum reform; and Peggy McIntosh's (1989) discussion of privilege.

### Summary of the Conceptual Frameworks

Embracing the concept of diversity requires parity of partici-pation, and social justice requires arrangements that permit its members to interact with one another as equals (Fraser & Honneth, 2003). Two conditions prevent parity of participation (Fraser & Honneth, 2003, pp. 10–11): (1) Issues of redistribu-tion (the current distribution of resources, wealth, education, health care, and other assets) prevent equal participation. (2) Issues of recognition [the disrespect of identities and pressures to assimilate to dominate cultural norms (White male privilege) and the marginalization of racial, ethnic, gender, sexual, and ideological minorities prevent equal participation].

Two strategies are necessary to address non-parity of participation (Fraser & Honneth, 2003): (1) affirmative strategies that involve addressing and correcting the outcomes of injustices, and (2) transformative strategies that address injustices by restructuring the underlying cultural/social/political framework. I will term this framework the privilege structure that exists. Blackmore (2016) provides an overview of Fraser's work in relation to educational leadership. Education leadership and curriculum reform/transformation is critical to these strategies (Banks, 2003) as well as the understanding of privilege (McIntosh, 1989; Middleton, Anderson, & Banning, 2009).

## My Thoughts on Diversity and Organizations

For me, the diversity challenge of parity of participation in organization relates directly to the priviledge structure of White male gender. In weaving the following relationship between male gender and organizational behavior, the complexity of the relationship has been simplified in order to highlight the patterns. Several authors have provided for me key definitional elements for understanding gender and organizations. The following are noted: Elizabeth Dodson Grey's (1982) *Patriarch as a Conceptual Trap*; Ann Wilson Schaef (1985), who wrote *Women's Reality: An Emerging Female System in a White Male Society*, and Alfie Kohn (1992), the author of *No Contest: The Case Against Competition*. Each of these authors presents a set of myths that provide the socialization blueprint for gender roles in our society and the foundation for the White male system.

Elizabeth Dodson Gray (1982) suggests three myths:

1. Reality is construed to be hierarchical: to reinforce the construction of a hierarchical reality, everything in our society is ranked from the top twenty-five in various sporting events to the top pizza parlors in town. Ranking, according to Kohn (1986), is our national pastime.

2. Man is above nature: Man, or more specifically "men" are on top of the hierarchy and control nature. They assume

dominion over nature and use it for their purposes. Forests are cleared, dams are built, and the earth is plowed.

3. Nature is feminine: If nature is feminine, then it follows that our metaphors and analogies for nature are feminine. For example, Mother Nature, virgin forests, and raping the land. It also follows that if "men" control nature, then they control women. These three myths provide the hierarchical structure necessary for the domination of women and nature by men. Nowhere is this hierarchical structure so ingrained and more powerful than in organizations, including colleges and universities.

Ann Wilson Schaef (1985) suggests four myths that guide the gender socialization process:

1. The White male system is the only thing that exists.

2. The White male system is innately superior.

3. The White male system knows and understands everything.

4. The White male system believes that it is possible to be totally logical, rational, and objective.

These myths reinforce the notion that it is, indeed, the male gender that is on top of the hierarchy and is in control of the internal functioning of the organization.

Finally, Alfie Kohn (1986) suggests four myths that strike at the heart of what makes the White male system function:

1. Competition is an unavoidable fact of life and part of human nature.

2. Competition motivates man to do his best.

3. Competition provides a way to have fun and a good time.

4. Competition builds character and is good for self-confidence.

Although these competition myths are generally thought to be true by many, they are not supported by social/psychological research.

Taken as a whole, these three authors' myths provide the structure for the male socialization blueprint in our society. The myths underpin how males are socialized, how males are supposed to behave in organizations, and "how the organizational system" works in our society. The photographs that follow in this chapter were taken from the foregoing interpretative frame and from my personal experiences as a White, hetersexual, cisgender, abled-bodied, professional, middle-class male.

### References:

Banks, J. (2003). *An introduction to multicultural education.* 3rd ed. Boston: Allyn & Bacon.

Blackmore, J. (2016). *Educational leadership and Nancy Fraser (Critical studies in educational leadership, management, and administration).* London: Routledge.

Fraser, N., & Honneth, A. (2003). *Redistribution or recognition? A political-philosophical exchange.* London: Verso Publisher.

Grey, E. D. (1982). *Patriarch as a conceptual trap.* Wellesley, MA: Roundtable Press.

Kohn, A. (1992). *No contest: The case against competition.* Boston, MA: Houghton Mifflin.

McIntosh, P. (1989 July/August). White privilege. Unpacking the invisible backpack. *Peace and Freedom*, 8-10.

Middleton, V., Anderson, S., & Banning, J. (2009). The journey to understanding privilege: A meta-narrative approach. *Journal of Transformative Education, 7*(4), 294-311.

Quaye, S. J., & Harper, S. R. (Eds.). (2015*). Student engagement in higher education: Theoretical perspectives and practical approaches for diverse populations.* 2nd Ed. New York: Routledge.

Schaef, A. W. (1985). *Women's reality: An emerging female system in a White male society.* San Francisco, CA: Harper & Row.

Winkler-Wagner, R., & Locks, A. M. (2014). *Diversity and inclusion on campus: Supporting racially and ethnically underrepresented students.* New York: Routledge.

## Using the Eclectic Interpretative Frame for Understanding Diversity Messages

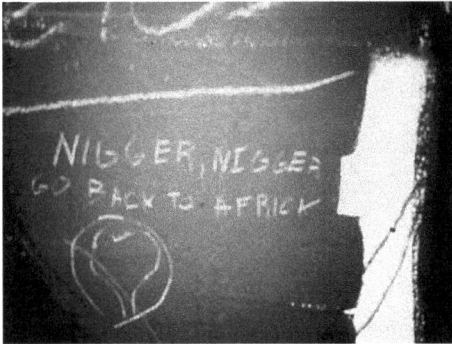

*Photo 3.1  Not Welcomed*

As noted in chapter two, the eclectic provides tools for understanding and interpreting the photographs of campus material culture. Implementation of this approach in this chapter is built around the process of asking questions of the material culture of interest regarding campus diversity. Answers to the following questions help in providing the information needed for forming the interpretation of the artifact and its relation to the messages of diversity. The interpretative frame regarding campus diversity is designed around asking the following questions.

### Basic Question: Are the Diversity Messages Manifest or Latent?

First, there is the basic question of whether the message of the artifact is manifest or latent (Neuendorf, 2002).

If manifest, then few questions need to be asked. The message is self-evident and obvious. Photo 3.1 is clearly manifest. There is no

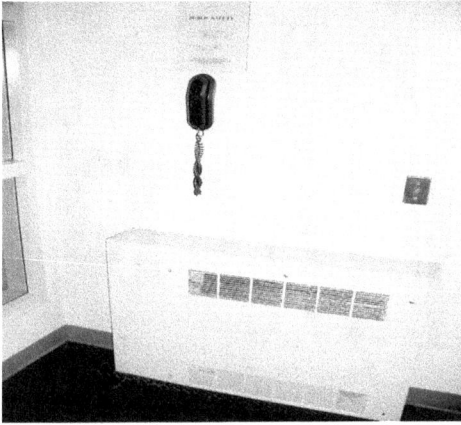

*Photo 3.2 Welcome*

*Photo 3.3 Binary Carpet*

need for further interpretive questions. African American students are not welcomed. The more the images fall in the direction of latent/ conative the greater the need for interpretive skills. Photo 3.2 needs only a bit more interpretation. The phone is an emergency phone, but its location makes it inaccessible to students who use wheelchairs to navigate the campus. Was the phone placed in its position without thought to students with disabilities? The camera will not answer this question, but a presentation of the photo to a campus group should stimulate interesting and important discussion. Are there issues on campus regarding the lack of attention to students with physical disabilities?

### Additional Questions: Tools for Deconstruction

*Does the photograph of the cultural artifact contain binary oppositions?*

Look for arrangement of elements in pairs (Emmison & Smith, 2000). Photo 3.3 shows new carpeting and old sixties flowered carpeting on the same floor. Further inspection indicated that the old carpeting was covering the hallway floor outside of the campus minority services offices while the new carpet was covering the hallway floor in front of the general student services offices, like the admissions office. A binary contrast can also include photographs of

*Photo 3.4  Use of Ladies*

*Photo 3.5  Foreground Background*

similar campus artifacts but not be contained in the same photo. For example, restroom signage is often not parallel: many campuses use the term "Men" to denote the men's restroom, but then use a different level of label for women's restrooms (see Photo 3.4).

*What is the relationship among the elements in the photograph in terms of foreground and background?*

The more "important" elements of the photograph appear as the foreground. For example, in Photo 3.5 we have both White and African American women (mannequin) in a campus neighborhood retail display. The White women are in the foreground while the African

*Photo 3.6  Posture Differences*

*Photo 3.7  Male Standing*

*Photo 3.8  Female Sitting*                    *Photo 3.9  Male in Dominate Stance*

American women are in the background (even difficult to see in the photo). Also note that the models do not have heads, just bodies to reflect sexual messages. Symbolism is an important aspect of all campus diversity photographs.

*What is the relationship among the people in the photograph in terms of body position?*

Messages of power in photographs are communicated by body position (Branaman, 2001; Emmison & Smith, 2000). Typically, the person standing is associated with more power than those sitting (Banning, Sexton, Most, & Maier, 2007). For example, Photo 3.6 is of a mural found on campus. The male is standing and female is kneeling. It is also a common practice that if statuary is dedicated to a male, he is often standing (Photo 3.7). Statuary dedicated to a female often takes the less powerful position of sitting (Photo 3.8). It is not unusual to see these positions of power depicted in a sculpture installation where the male is given a dominant role (see Photo 3.9). The boy is standing and the girl is sitting.

*What is the relationship among the overt public messages given via institutional publications—for example, institutional advertisements, mission statements, recruitment materials, etc.—and the messages found in the cultural artifacts?*

As noted in chapter two, many campuses use photographs of groups of students engaged in a variety of activities that include a wide

*Photo 3.10  Washington Carver*

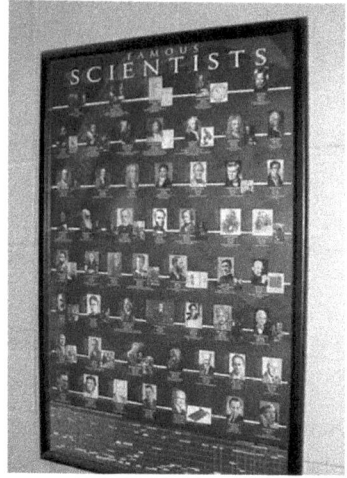

*Photo 3.11  No Carver*

array of students in their promotional brochures. But in real life on campus, such multiracial activity is seldom apparent. Photo 3.10 is from an institutional effort to promote the contributions of an African American scientist, but George Washington Carver's photo is nowhere to be found in the science department poster of famous scientists (Photo 3.11). The binary description of what is being displayed by the university and what is being done "on the ground," so to speak, is clearly present.

*What roles are depicted in the artifact photograph, and to what person are they assigned? What roles are missing for specific groups?*

Photo 3.12 is a mural identifying and depicting a campus dental program. Men have the roles of dentist and an

*Photo 3.12  Dental Program Mural*

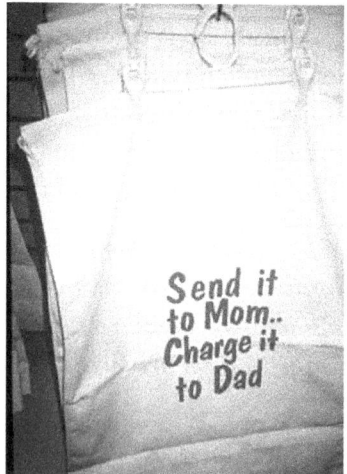

*Photo 3.13  Clothing Bag*

administrator, and women are "dental assistants" and patient—a clear binary in power and status.

In Photo 3.13, gender roles are clearly stated on the bag being sold in the campus bookstore to transport dirty laundry. "Send it to Mom—charge it to Dad." The message is that Mom does house chores like washing clothes, but Dad makes the money.

*What symbols and associated meanings are included in the artifact photograph?*

Photo 3.14  Praying Hands

Photo 3.15  White Traditional Family

The artifacts of campus material culture send symbolic messages (Gagliardi, 1990). The presences of the "praying hands" in Photo 3.14 symbolizes the institution's faith-based mission.

Photo 3.15 is symbolizing "family," but the symbol only captures traditional family configurations—mother, father, and child. The numerous other family arrangements in our culture are not represented, and the plaque reads: "The University Family." This configuration of family is not "universal."

*Does the artifact photograph suggest a narrative?*

Does the photograph or the series of photographs tell a story? Is there a story line (Emmison and Smith, 2000)? For example, an academic department will often have a series of murals depicting

Photo 3.16 American Indian Culture

Photo 3.17 Latino Hispanic Culture

Photo 3.18 White Culture

Photo 3.19 Working Together

the history of their discipline. Within the series, typically there are stories imbedded regarding race and ethnicity. The four murals in a university library were painted to represent the three major cultures of the region—American Indian, Latino, and White. Photos 3.16, 3.17, and 3.18 represent these three cultures. Two are presented in a more historical context. The American Indian presentation (Photo 3.16) is associated with tepees, weaving, sheep herding, and basketry. These activities reflect the rich historical context of the American Indian, but little is present that captures a more contemporary scene. Photo 3.17 representing Latino/Hispanic culture of the Southwest continues the historical narrative. It depicts again, in a historical context, the Southwest Hispanic culture, highlighting the role of the Catholic Church, manual labor in the fields, and the use of adobe for house building. White culture (Photo 3.18), however, departs from the historical/traditional narrative and suggests it is within White culture that you find scientists and physicians, with stars and sun in the background. For campus students in the library, the three photographs do not share the same prospects for the future. It is only White culture that offers professional vocational opportunities. This change in narrative discrepancy is further reinforced by the last mural in the series of four. Photograph 3.19 is described by the mural painter as showing the three cultures working together. However, the centrality of the White figure can be interpreted as "upfront, central, and important" while the other two cultures are shown as side attractions.

The working together is the messages contained in the "holding of hands," but as one of my astute Hispanic workshop students pointed out, the hands are being held in a very awkward position. The hands are being held in such a manner that if the White male moves forward, the other two persons representing the American Indian and Latino/Hispanic culture must fall or move backward. My insightful student then remarked: "And that is the history of our culture."

*Do the elements of the "Behavioral/Physical Traces" observational method (Zeisel, 1975, 1981, 2006) help in the interpretation of the cultural artifact?*

Photo 3.20 Foreplay Erosion

The behavioral trace method is built on the notion that as we use cultural artifacts in our environment, there are traces of that use or behavior that can be detected. These behavioral traces can be interpreted as non-verbal messages that increase the understanding of campus behavior and can be photographed (Banning, 1988). Zeisel's work focuses on four types of behavioral/physical trace categories. The *by-product of use* category includes the messages of erosion, leftovers, missing traces, and accretions. For example, in Photo 3.20, erosion of the paint in the female's pubic area suggests touching by students as

Photo 3.21  Female Figure

Photo 3.22  Obstruction

they pass by the mural on their fourth floor residence hall. The "Happiness is Fourplay" caption on the mural is supportive of this interpretation.

The concept of accretion or build-up of material is captured in Photo 3.21. The female figure is standing, which is not often found, but the figure has been covered with foreign materials, and there is also trace evidence that signs have been posted on the figure. The summary interpretation of the photograph suggests that the female figure has been molested and that the diversity message is females may be unsafe on campus.

The missing traces concept is also useful in developing interpretation. Members of diversity groups are often missing in campus flyers and other printed material.

The category of *adaptation of use* shows how the artifacts of the campus are moved, connected, and separated by behavioral use. In Photo 3.22, a waste receptacle has been moved to block the handicapped curb access to the campus. Was it placed at the position of obstruction by intention or by accident? Regardless of the motivation, no one has taken the time or effort to move the receptacle.

The third category is *displays of self* that captures how we use the physical artifacts in the processes of personalization and identification and in communicating group membership. Photo 3.23 is a student mural painted for the purpose of personalizing and identifying the

*Photo 3.23  Integration*

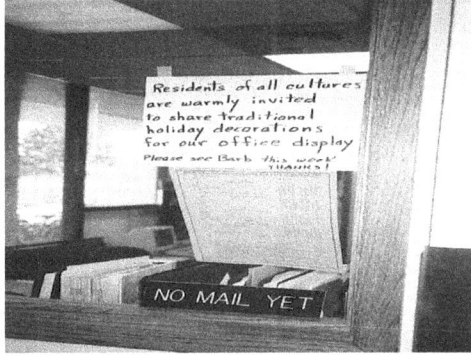

*Photo 3.24 All  Cultures Invited*

ninth floor of a residence hall, but there is much more to the mural. Often, you find Black male students are given numbered shirts, as if all Black students are a part of an athletic program on campus. In this particular photo, the scene includes a White female and a Black male standing in front of urinals with the caption of "Let's Integrate.." The context of the photograph degrades the concept of integration and takes away from serious thought and discussion regarding the concept.

Photo 3.24 illustrates the personalization of a residence hall that sends the message that all cultures are included. All residents have group membership in the community celebration.

Finally, the last category is *public messages*. Three types of messages are described: official, unofficial, and illegitimate. The category of illegitimate includes graffiti. Graffiti is the most prevalent and often contains the most negative and hurtful diversity messages. For example, Photo 3.25 shows bathroom graffiti that uses a slang term to "rule out" members of the lesbian community. Likewise, Photo

*Photo 3.25  Bathroom Graffiti*

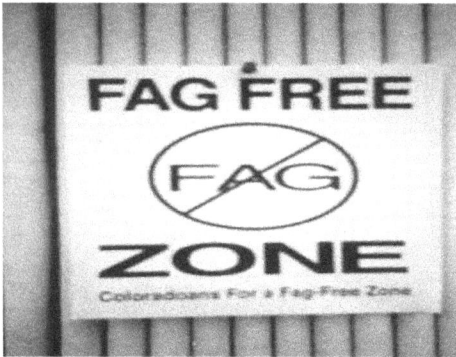

Photo 3.26  Unofficial Sign

3.26 sends a similar message—not in graffiti form but in an unofficial form—to the gay community. (See Appendix A for a full description of the Zeisel observational method with non-diversity related examples and photo illustrations.)

**Moving from Individual Photos to Cultural Themes**

Developing an understanding of campus cultural themes from a group of individual photographs is basically a task of qualitative data analysis. In qualitative data analysis, the approach of moving from observational data to larger themes falls within two major strategies: inductive and deductive. The inductive approach is a data driven approach where the movement to larger themes is built on assigning codes/labels to individual data and then comparing the codes to move up the ladder of abstraction to reach themes (Corbin & Strauss, 2008). The deductive approach brings to the observational data categories/themes already having been established by previous research or theory (Boyatzis, 1998). Useful to developing themes from individual photographs is using a combination of both the inductive and the deductive strategies. This combination strategy is termed "template analysis" (King, 1998). In this approach, deductive or prior codes/categories are established, but inductive or codes driven by the data are added as needed.

Taxonomies are useful tools in establishing prior codes/categories to assist in moving from the individual photos to cultural themes. The concept of taxonomy is typically noted as stemming from Greek concepts for denoting a method of arranging and is used today to describe a method to group things together. The purpose of a taxonomy (Milgram & Kishino, 1994) is to present an ordered classification system that allows and promotes discussions that can be focused, developments evaluated, research conducted, and data meaningfully compared. Taxonomies can be developed inductively, or if they exist, they can be imported from previous scholarship/research or theory.

Banning and Bartels (1997) developed a taxonomy for classifying campus artifact messages. This taxonomy has four dimensions: (1) the content of the message, (2) the evaluative impact of the message, (3) multicultural groups, and (4) the type of physical artifact sending the message.

By using this classification taxonomy, each photograph of campus physical artifacts can be assigned to a cell in the taxonomy, and the questions of which artifacts are communicating what message to what groups with what results can be addressed. The categories for content of photograph messages in Banning and Bartels' taxonomy include: (1) messages of belonging, (2) messages of safety, (3) messages of equality, and (4) messages regarding roles. The artifacts may send multiple messages, and a single photograph may belong to more than one category. The evaluative impact dimension of photographs included two categories: (1) overtly negative and (2) overtly positive. The multicultural group dimension included: (1) gender, (2) race and ethnicity, (3) ethnicity, (4) religion, and (5) sexual orientation. The type of artifacts generating the messages included: (1) architecture; physical structures and design elements of the campus (2) art; including paintings, murals, posters, (3) signs; signs fall within several categories, including official signs, unofficial signs, and illegitimate signs, and (4) graffiti; often viewed as an illegitimate sign, but because of its ubiquitous nature on campus, it is given separate status in the classification system.

In 2008, the Banning and Bartels' taxonomy's category of evaluative content of the message was expanded to include the following evaluations: negative, null, contributive, and transformational (Banning, Middleton, & Dennison, 2008). The negative label is assigned to both manifest and latent photographs where the message is clearly discriminatory and produces a hostile climate for students of diversity. The null category was derived from the work of Freeman (1979) and Betz (1989) and captures the circumstances when a campus has an absence of negative, but yet no positives. Without affirming and sending positive messages, the campus does not remain neutral. This is similar to the concept of "White silence" (DiAngelo, 2016). Being ignored or left out creates a negative environment not from what is said, but what is not said. The contributive and transformational categories were built on the work of Banks (2003). The contributive category captures positive messages, but the messages are presented without the call for personal involvement to bring about change. The placement of a Martin Luther King portrait in the campus library certainly sends a positive message and contributes to diversity, but it does not call for personal involvement or discussion with others. The transformative message is also positive, but calls for a personal commitment to transform campus culture. For example, a poster depicting the need for volunteers to work with minority youth and providing the necessary information to become involved would be categorized as transformative.

Figure 3.1 depicts another variation of a taxonomy built on the previous two and is related to theory as the deductive base for the messages of equality. Strange and Banning (2015) theorize that for students to be successful in their campus experience they should feel welcomed, safe, included, and, therefore, a part of the campus community. The notions of welcoming, safety, inclusion, and community become the artifact messages critical to the success of students. In addition, to allow for the taxonomy to be inductive as well, the multicultural group dimension includes "additional." For example, the additional category could include a focus on veterans or diversity issues associated with urban and rural students.

In summary, each picture of an artifact type (art, signs, graffiti, and architecture) would fit into one or more of the cells of the taxonomy (see Figure 3.1). The taxonomy includes the equity groups to which the artifact message references (gender, race, ethnicity, religion, sexual orientation, physical, and additional), the content of the message includes (welcoming, safety, inclusion, and community), and the equity approach is represented by the artifact messages of (negative, null, contributions/additive, and transformational/social action).

Photo illustrations of the concepts of welcoming, safety, inclusion, and community are presented in the next section.

*Figure 3.1*

**A Taxonomy for Diversity Photographs**

**Type of Artifact**

| Art | Signs | Graffiti | Architecture |

**Equity Parameters**

**Equity Approach**

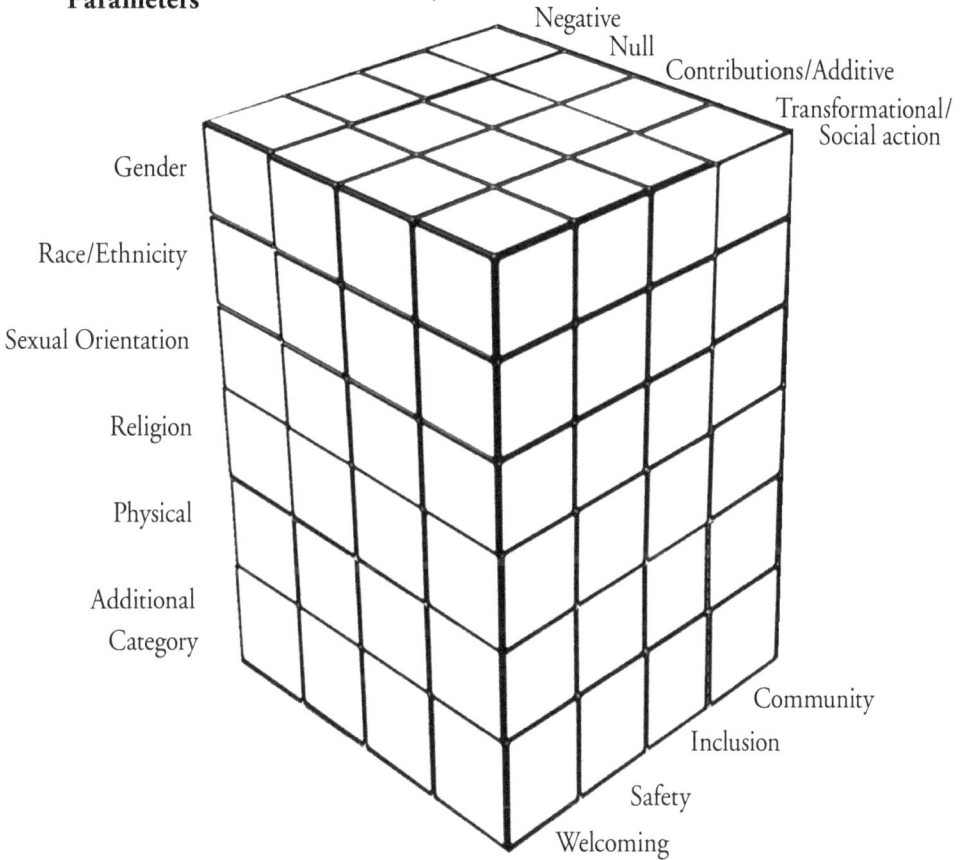

Negative
Null
Contributions/Additive
Transformational/
Social action

Gender

Race/Ethnicity

Sexual Orientation

Religion

Physical

Additional
Category

Community
Inclusion
Safety
Welcoming

**Message Content**

## Photo Illustrations of Message Content: Welcoming, Safety, Inclusion, and Community

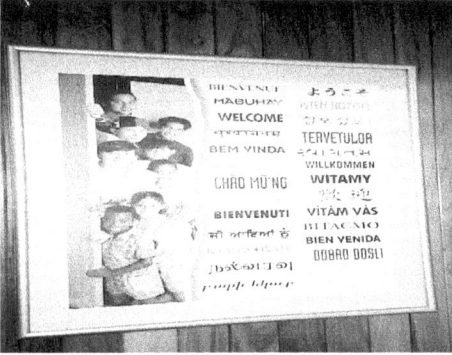

*Photo 3.27  A Diversity of Welcome*

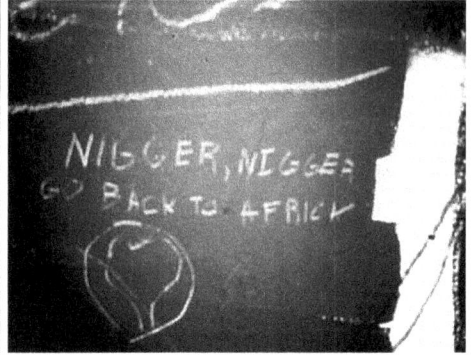

*Photo 3.28  Go Back to Africa*

*Photo 3.29*
*Non Welcome to Gay Community*

*Photo 3.30  Walk Bikes*

*Welcoming*

Photographs 3.27 to 3.30 illustrate issues associated with welcoming students of diversity. Photo 3.27 (a union building welcome sign) clearly suggests all are welcomed to campus. Photo 3.28 sends a message specific to African American students that they are not welcome and should return to Africa. Photo 3.29 is of a sign on a meeting door and sends a non-welcoming message to the gay community. It states "FAG FREE ZONE" and indicates an entire state is supportive of the message. Photo 3.30 sends a very physical non-welcoming message to the students who use wheelchairs for mobility. The pipes were intended to slow bike traffic, but the message is clear. Wheelchairs cannot enter the campus.

*Photo 3.31  Low Clearance Safety Issue*

*Photo 3.32  Low Clearance Safety Issue*

*Photo 3.33  Asphalt for Curb Cut Safety*

*Photo 3.34  Trash Can Blockage*

The theme of safety can also be captured by photographs. Photo 3.31 presents a major safety issue for all visually impaired who are six feet four inches tall or taller and travel the campus. The signage reads "Low Clearance 6'4"" which is of no help for the visually impaired using a cane to help in navigating the buildings and walkways of the campus. The same error in design can be seen in Photos 3.32. An unsafe "curb cut" for access is presented in Photo 3.33. In addition to the physical dangers for the students who use alternative mobility methods on campus, the message of "we did not expect you, and we did not do our best in welcoming you and making the campus pathways safe for

*Photo 3.35  Defacing Female Statue*

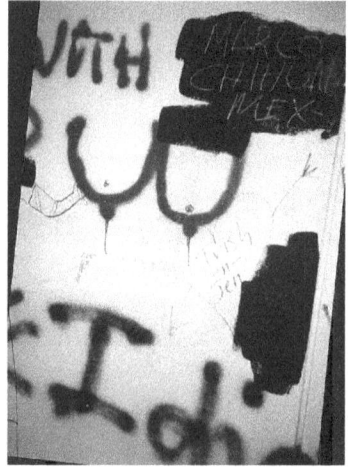

*Photo 3.36*
*Bleeding Breast Graffiti*

you" is also conveyed. The message is one of "afterthought" and "make do." The message of "unsafe" is sent in Photo 3.34 despite the proper curb cut. The trash container prevents the safe use of access. Again, in addition to the physical message of unsafe access, the user of the curb cut can only wonder who is responsible for the dangerous arrangement. Is it an oversight on the part of the institution or is it intended to be a deliberately unwelcoming message for some individual or group?

It is not only the students with disabilities who are presented unsafe messages by the campus artifacts, but other groups are also subjected to messages that raise questions regarding safety. Photo 3.35 sends an unsafe message for women on campus. The standing woman has been the target of paint vandalism, and there are traces of "signs" of some nature having been attached to her body. One observer of the photograph called the results of these behaviors "molestation." Likewise, Photo 3.36 of campus graffiti depicts "bleeding breasts" on a tunnel wall connecting to adjacent sections of campus.

Campuses have begun to recognize the importance of "feeling safe" for students of diversity and are establishing "safe zones." These zones are most often program offices and individual offices. Photo 3.37 is an example found on a faculty office door.

Photo 3.37 Safe Zone

*Inclusion*

Inclusion is a more abstract concept than welcoming and safety, but inclusionary messages do exist. Many

Photo 3.38
Stalls with Half Doors

times, the non-inclusionary messages are ones that suggest that certain diversity groups cannot be unconditionally included and their behaviors warrant surveillance. This dynamic is particularly found in campus restrooms. Photo 3.38 shows half restroom stall doors. These were in a building housing academic programs stereotypically associated with gay men. The purpose of the half-doors was to provide visual surveillance of behaviors within stalls. This is clearly a strategy built on ignorance, stereotypical thinking, and the lack of full inclusion of gay men without "conditional measures" to campus. Again, in Photo 3.39 the message on the restroom door expects unacceptable

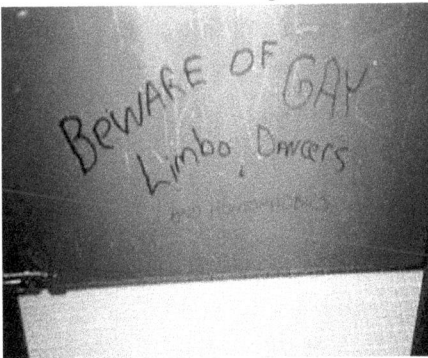

Photo 3.39 Restroom Door Message

behaviors of gay men, ruling out full inclusion. The message of "Beware of Gay Limbo Dancers" suggests gay men are looking under the bathroom stall door. The additional word below this message is "& homophobic." Restroom graffiti often serves as a method of asynchronous communication

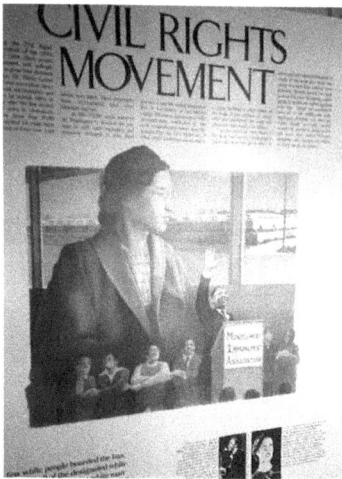

Photo 3.40
Civil Rights movement

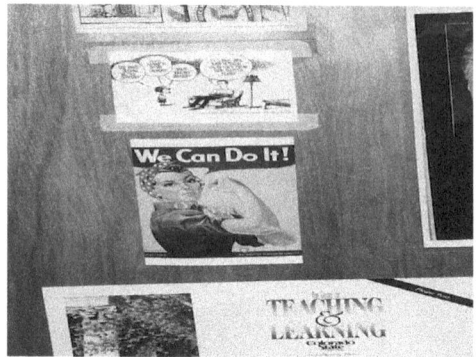

Photo 3.41  Women Included

about important issues of diversity. A forum for a campus dialogue about these issues would be an important next programmatic step.

Positive inclusionary artifacts also exist on campuses. The civil rights movement poster in Photo 3.40 signals that the history of diversity and the importance of civil rights for all is a part of the campus cultural artifacts. Likewise, Photo 3.41 sends a "you are included" motivational message for women.

The mobility-disabled student is also sent messages of inclusion when buildings are accessible and handicapped entrances are clearly marked and fully usable. Too often bicycles are chained to handicapped ramp rails, making it difficult for the user to feel fully accepted and included by all. There are clear messages around inclusion and non-inclusion for the mobility-impaired student located at academic departmental offices. These offices often place departmental information, advising information, and other forms that students need outside the office door. However, the forms are often difficult, if not impossible, to reach for the mobility impaired. They must find help (see Photo 3.42). This height arrangement sends a message of non-inclusion, but some campuses recognize this issue and send a strong and clear message that the forms are accessible to students in wheelchairs. (See photo 3.43, in which forms are available at doorknob level.

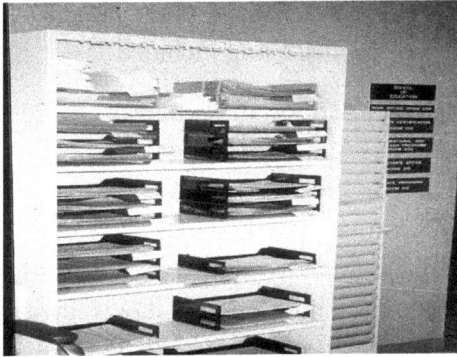

*Photo 3.42  Information too High*

*Photo 3.43 Door Knob Level Information*

*Community*

Campus artifacts can also send messages that focus on community. Again, like inclusionary messages, they are often more abstract, and non-community messages are often more easily captured due to their usual manifest nature. Photo 3.44 does send a community message to a residence hall by signaling to all that "Residents of all cultures are warmly invited to share traditional holiday decorations for our office display." Photo 3.27 gives a welcome to a wide range of diverse cultures, which forms the foundation for the concept of community—all are included. Non-community messages suggest groups are being left out. Not all members of the community are being included. This is clear in the K-12 Photo 3.45, where the "right class" is White

*Photo 3.44  Resident Community*

*Photo 3.45  Right Class*

Photo 3.46  Male Library Symbol

with no sense of the larger community being included.

An important concept to understanding campus culture and material artifacts is social norming (Berkowitz, 2003). Photographs can assist in this effort. Photo 3.46 shows a concrete sculptured male figure attached to the library wall reading a book. In addition to the message that females may not be included in the library, a campus narrative has been established regarding the male figure. The story is that he will turn a page in his book each time a female virgin enters the library. This artifact and narrative sends a normative message that all women on campus are sexually active. A false norm can influence sexual behaviors in the community.

Many campuses have similar myths associated with material artifacts: statues of soldiers holding rifles will shoot when a female virgin walks by, metal birds will fly from the campus fountain, and bricks will fall from the campus clock tower when a female virgin passes. All these examples produce a "false norm" message for the campus community regarding sexual behavior. A false norm is, in fact, not the norm, but it influences behaviors. In these cases, not all females on campus are sexually active, but the artifact messages continue to send that false norm message.

**Collection and Utilization of Diversity Photographs**

Previously in this chapter, the importance of the role of interpretation and the illustrations of diversity photographs were presented. To complete the chapter, the collection of photographs will be presented along with analysis of how to utilize the photographs in the examination and enhancement of campus culture for diversity. Key to both the collection and utilization of diversity photographs is participation. Full participation of all campus members is critical to both the collection and utilization. Many of the negative and problematic photos presented earlier in this chapter illustrate the problems when individuals and individual offices place artifacts in the campus environment without meaningful discussion with diverse groups.

For example, the line of pipes erected to slow bike traffic (Photo 3.30) would never have been installed if a student or staff representing the mobility impaired who use wheelchairs had been present for the discussion of the design. Much of the gender-related statuary would also have taken a different form if full participation included the campus offices and programs serving women. This broad participation from campus constituencies is needed to address existing negative issues, to prevent new negative artifacts from appearing, and to support positive diversity artifacts in the campus culture. The following strategies for collection and utilization of photographs all embrace the importance of participation.

**Strategies for Collection and Participation.**

*Solo Strategies*

Solo strategies for the collection of photographs can take two forms: (1) using an outside consultant, and (2) solo inhabitants from the campus. There are advantages and disadvantages to using an outside consultant. An outsider can bring a "fresh" set of eyes for observation and perhaps see and understand artifact messages that on-campus personnel have become so accustomed to that they fail to see. However, at the same time, the outsider does not have a full understanding of campus history. To lessen this disadvantage yet use the expertise and training of an outside consultant, the consulting role can move toward training. For example, local campus personnel can be trained on how to recognize and interpret campus artifacts relating to diversity. The trained individuals can then begin the collection of photographs for campus discussion. The consultant's expertise is utilized, but the participation of the campus is ensured through training.

A second solo strategy is to recruit and designate individual students and staff to collect photographs as they encounter the campus environment in their daily routines. The individual photographs can be sent to a central depository site for collection and presentation for group discussion—again ensuring campus participation and discussion.

An important advantage of having individuals collect photographs during their normal activities on campus is that they can initiate immediate action if they find disturbing artifacts. For example, a class field trip to photograph a university library found that a considerable number of the book return carts had been vandalized with graffiti. Photographs of the graffiti were not held for discussion, but immediate notification was made to the library staff. Currently, many campuses have a twenty-four-hour graffiti removal policy. Having designated individuals taking photographs puts more "hands-on-deck" with critical information to start the removal process. (See Shade Box 3-2.) Photographs gathered by the solo photographers that raise questions regarding interpretation can be gathered for presentation and discussion at a variety of group gatherings, thereby ensuring participation of the campus.

### Shade Box 3-2: Removal of Campus Artifacts

The campus artifacts that include hate messages and are presented in the form of graffiti should be removed immediately; however, historical campus artifacts that send negative messages (statuary, murals, paintings, and monuments) and, in some manner, are "institutionalized" present a more complex decision process. Important ingredients to consider in the decision-making process regarding removal are the following:

• Most critical: the decision-making discussion process should include all campus groups.

- Discussion should address the important issues regarding the ethics of social intervention (Kelman & Warwick, 1978) in addition to the full participation of the community.

  - Who will benefit and who will not benefit from the decision of removal?

  - What methods will be used to implement the decision of removal?

  - Who will monitor the process and outcomes of the removal?

- If the campus retains an artifact that has a negative message for diversity rather than removal, the artifact needs to become transformational. Information regarding the artifact (history, purpose, importance, controversies, disagreements, etc.) needs to be placed near the artifact for public viewing and invite public thought and comment. The artifact becomes transformational in that it becomes an invitation for educational and personal thought. The placing of the issues of the artifact for public viewing and thought sends an important message that the campus values community dialogue and does not accept "White Silence" (DiAngelo, 2016) but promotes open and difficult discussions regarding matters of diversity.

*Group Strategies*

Campuses can find many group strategies for the collection and utilization of diversity photographs, but two strategies will be highlighted: (1) group field trips gathering photographs and (2) group projects related to academic coursework. Group field trips highlights the simple procedure of designated campus groups engaging in field trip–like activities to gather photographs to present to various groups for discussion and action, if necessary.

The second group strategy is like the described group field trip, but the activity is designed as a part of an academic class project. For example, a graduate course in student affairs in a higher education program included the study of the campus environment. A project related to this curriculum goal was designed using the camera. Students were assigned different parking lots on campus to collect photographs of bumper stickers. The resulting photo collection was utilized for discussion to discover what cultural interests and values were being displayed. (See Shade Box 3-3.) The solo and group strategies for the collection and utilization of diversity photographs are not restricted to the ones briefly discussed above. Many opportunities for creative processes exist, but critical to all strategies is the concept of campus participation.

**Shade Box 3-3: Bumper Sticker Ethnography**

**Bumper Sticker Ethnography: Another Way to View the Campus Ecology**

*Ethnography*

The focus of ethnographic inquiry is on answering the question: "What is the culture of this group of people" (Patton, 1990). Traditionally, the method of choice was for the ethnographer to "live in" the culture as a participant observer and collect information about the culture through interviews, observations, and documents. Banning (1991) points out the usefulness of the ethnographic approach in an attempt to understand the culture of the campus, and the notion of a campus cultural audit has been well documented (Kuh and Whitt, 1988; Whitt, 1993; Whitt and Kuh, 1991). Whitt (1993) defined a culture audit as providing "both insiders and outsiders with a means to systematically discover and identify the artifacts, values, and assumptions that comprise an organization's culture" (p. 83). Kuh and Whitt (1988) note that cultural assumptions and beliefs "... are just below the surface ... manifested in observable forms or artifacts" (p. 16). Geertz (1973) suggests a similar notion, that artifacts store cultural meaning. Banning and Bartels (in press) illustrate how photographs of cultural artifacts (artwork, posters, sculpture, physical structures, and graffiti) can help evaluate the multicultural "attitude" of a campus. The purpose of that article is to illustrate the potential of using "bumper stickers" as a campus cultural artifact to assist in the understanding of the campus culture or ecology.

### Bumper Stickers

Carol Gardner (1995), in her book *Bumper Sticker Wisdom: America's Pulpit above the Tailpipe,* shares many important observations about bumper stickers. She notes that bumper stickers lead to a portrait of America "... a nation of people in automobiles—that ultimate national icon—on the move with stickers expressing a view, sharing a frustration, or offering some perceived insight, solution, or wisdom" (p. 6). She goes on to note:

> The bumper sticker may be an expression of personal philosophy, political anger and outrage, religious conviction, parental pride, sexual preference, or social comment. It may represent a simple statement of personal humor, ethnic identity, or class resentment. It may offer views of the opposite sex and marriage or of American culture and social institutions. (p. 6.)

Gardner (1995) also points this out: "... bumper stickers do not emerge in a vacuum but with the era and political culture of which they are a part" (p. 6). Can the aggregate of campus bumper stickers be another way to view the campus culture or ecology? The following are photographs of some of the bumper stickers found on a college campus in the Rocky Mountain West. The major themes of the culture suggested by the bumper stickers are: (1) environmental issues and conflicts, (2) religious issues and conflicts, (3) sexual orientation issues, (4) political issues, (5) abortion issues, (6) violence issues, and (7) individualistic expressions.

*Summary*

The foregoing illustrates the potential of using campus bumper stickers as a way to understand campus culture. Several different approaches can be taken. The approach presented in this shade box leads to a general view of the campus culture built on the notion of taking photographs of all the bumper stickers on campus—an aggregate approach. A number of comparative approaches could also be implemented. For example, a comparison could be made between student bumper stickers and faculty bumper stickers. Perhaps generational differences might appear. Another possibility would be to compare stickers among student groups. How do the commuter parking lot bumper stickers compare to the ones in residence hall parking lots? Do stickers reflect academic majors? How do the stickers in the community parking lots (shopping malls, etc.) compare to the ones on campus? Many possibilities exist. Bumper sticker ethnography may not present the most refined picture of the campus ecology, but it is another way to view the campus culture—a fun way at that!

## References:

Banning, J. H. (1991). Ethnography: A promising method of inquiry for the study of campus ecology. *The Campus Ecologist, 9*(3), 1-3.

Banning, J. H. & Bartels, S. (1997). A taxonomy: Campus physical artifacts as communicators of campus multicultural-ism. *NASPA Journal, 35*(1), 29-37. Washington. D. C.: National Association for Student Personnel Administrators.

Gardner, C. W. (I 995). *Bumper sticker wisdom: America's pulpit above the tailpipe.* Hillsboro, OR: Beyond Words Publishing Co.

Geertz, C. (l 973). *The interpretation of culture.* New York: Basic Books.

Kuh, G. D. & Whitt, E. J. (1988). The invisible tapestry: Cultures in American colleges and universities. *ASHE-ERIC Higher Education Report, No. 1.* Washington. D.C. Association for the Study of Higher Education.

Patton, M. (I 990). *Qualitative evaluation and research methods.* Newbury Park, CA: Sage Publishing.

Whitt, E. J. (1993). Making the familiar strange: Discovering culture. In G. D. Kuh (Ed.). *Cultural perspectives in student affairs work* (pp. 81-94). Washington, D.C. American College Personnel Association.

Whitt, E. J. & Kuh, G. D. (1991). The use of qualitative methods in a team approach to multiple institution studies. *The Review of Higher Education, 14,* 317-337. Revised from *The Campus Ecologist,* Vol. XIV No.3 1996.

**Ethical Issues: Photographing Campus Artifacts**

To leave the discussion of ethical issues to the closing of the manuscript does not suggest its lack of importance, but its juxtaposition to collection and utilization of photographs is important. Participation of others in all the aspects of photographing campus diversity messages is the critical ethical message, but there are also practical guidelines to be noted. (See Mitchell, C. M., 2011 Chapter Two: "On a pedagogy of ethics in visual research: Who's in the picture? for a very complete discussion of ethical issues.) I use the following simple guidelines in my instructions to campus groups and in class-related activities as they collect and utilize photographs.

- Typically, the photographs should be of a physical aspect of a public place in the campus environment, and people should not be included.

- If the desired photograph is in private spaces (offices, residence hall rooms, etc.), then permission to photograph must be obtained from the "owner" of the space. The owner should be given an opportunity to view the photograph and information as to how the photograph will be used prior to giving consent.

- If the desired photograph includes people, permission from the persons must be obtained. The resulting photograph must be reviewed by those people, and an explanation must be given to those participating of how it is to be used. For example, you would indicate the photographs are being collected as an assignment in a graduate class studying the campus environment, and that they may be shared with campus administrators and/or used in publications relating to the campus environment.

- Finally, remember: no photograph is worth the invasion of someone's privacy.

**Summary**

The purpose of this book is to present a short practical approach on how to photograph diversity messages on campus. The scholarship lines of the ecological perspective, material culture, and visual/photographic research provide the connection to key conceptual and research efforts that are supportive of this very practical endeavor of photographing campus culture. Tools of interpretation are provided to assist in discovering the possible diversity messages attached to campus artifacts.

Social justice must be the foundation of the educational enterprise, and our campus artifacts must include the welcome, safety, and inclusion of all to develop community. To help ensure these conditions, we must understand the diversity messages of campus artifacts. We can photograph, interpret, and change these messages—enhancing the positive and changing the negative. The aim of this practical approach to campus diversity is to have the camera on campus contribute to the historical relationship between photography and social justice.

## References:

Banks, J. (2003). *An introduction to multicultural education.* 3rd ed. Boston: Allyn & Bacon.

Banning, J. H. (1988). Behavioral traces: A concept for campus ecologists. *The Campus Ecologist, 6*(2), 1,3.

Banning, J. H. (1996). Bumper sticker ethnography: Another way to view the campus ecology. *The Campus Ecologist, 14*(3), 1-4.

Banning, J. H. & Bartels, S. (1997). A taxonomy: Campus physical artifacts as communicators of campus multiculturalism. *NASPA Journal, 35*(1), 29-37.

Banning, J. H., Middleton, V. & Dennison, T. (2008). Using photographs to assess equity climate: A taxonomy. *Multicultural Perspectives, 10*(1), 41-46.

Banning, J. H., Sexton, J., Most, D. E., & Maier, S. (2007). Gender asymmetries encountered in the search and exploration of mining engineering program websites: A portrayal of posture and roles. *Journal of Women and Minorities in Science and Engineering, 13*, 165-174.

Berkowitz, A. D. (2003). Applications of social norms theory to other health and social justice issues. In H.W. Perkins (Ed.)., *The social norm approach to preventing school and college age substance abuse: A handbook for educators, counselors, clinicians,* (pp.259-279). San Francisco: Jossey-Bass.

Betz, N. E. (1989). Implications of the null environment hypothesis for women's career development and for counseling psychology. *The Counseling Psychologist, 17*(1), 136–44.

Boyatzis, R. E. (1998). *Transforming qualitative information: Thematic analysis and code development.* Thousand Oaks, CA: Sage Publications.

Branaman, A. (Ed.). (2001). *Self and society.* New York: Blackwell Publishers.

Corbin, J., & Strauss, A. (2008). *Basics of qualitative research.* Los Angeles, CA: Sage.

DiAngelo, R. (2016). *What does it mean to be White?: Developing White racial literacy* New York: W.W. Norton & Co.

Emmison, M., & Smith, P. (2000). Researching the visual. London: Sage Publications.

Freeman, J. (1979). How to discriminate against women without really trying. In J. Freeman (Ed.). *Women: A feminist perspective* (pp. 194–208). Palo Alto, CA: Mayfield.

Gagliardi, P. (Ed.). (1990). *Symbols and artifacts: Views of the corporate landscape.* New York: Adline de Gruyter.

Kelman, H., & Warwick, D. (1978). The ethics of social intervention: Goals, means consequences. In G. Bemant, H. Kelman, & D. Warwick (Eds.). *The ethics of social intervention* (pp. 3-33). New York: Wiley and Sons.

King, N. (1998). Template analysis. In G. Symon & C. Cassell (Eds.). *Qualitative methods and analysis in organizational research: A practical guide* (pp. 118-134). Thousand Oaks, CA: Sage Publications.

Milgram, P., & Kishino, F. (1994). A taxonomy of mixed reality visual displays. *IEICE Transactions on Information Systems, E77-D* (12). Retrieved from http://vered.rose.utoronto.ca/people/paul_dir?IEIC94/ieice.html

Mitchell, C. (2011). *Doing visual research.* Los Angeles: Sage Publications.

Neuendorf, K. A. (2002). *The content analysis guidebook.* Thousand Oaks, CA: Sage Publications.

Ragin, C. C. (2008). *Redesigning social inquiry: Fuzzy sets and beyond*. Chicago: Chicago University Press.

Strange, C. C., & Banning, J. H. (2015). *Designing for learning: Creating campus environments for student success*. San Francisco, CA: Jossey-Bass.

Zeisel, J. (1975). *Sociology and architectural design*. Russell Sage Social Science Frontiers Series, No 6. New York: Free Press.

Zeisel, J. (1981). *Inquiry by design*: Monterey, CA: Brooks/Cole.

Zeisel, J. (2006). *Inquiry by design: Environment/behavior/ neuroscience in architecture, interiors, landscape, and planning*. New York: W. W. Norton & Company.

# APPENDIX A

Appendix A is a compilation and editing of several articles previously published in *The Campus Ecologist* (http://www.campusecologist.com). Photographs have been added to illustrate the use of the behavioral/physical trace approach.

## Material Culture, Behavior, and the Physical Trace Approach to Assessment

Discussion of the topic of behavior and the built material environment often starts by referring to the Winston Churchill statement that we shape our buildings and then they shape us. This observation leads to the question of what role material culture plays in student behavior. This question can be pursued from an ecological perspective by looking at the major issue embedded in the architecture/building and behavior relationship.

## Nature of Influence

The major issue that needs to be addressed is the nature of the influence that material culture in general and buildings in specific may have on behavior. In the literature, the nature of this influence has been conceptualized by three positions (Bell, Fisher, Baum, & Greene, 1990; Porteus, 1977). First, *architectural determinism* suggests that there is a rather direct and causal link between the built environment and behavior. A second position, environmental *or architectural possibilism* views the building as one that offers opportunities and sets limits for behavior. This relationship is denoted by context rather than determinism. Finally, environmental or *architectural probabilism* assumes that certain behaviors have probabilistic links to the built environment.

While all three positions offer insight into the relationship between material culture and behavior, to assume the position of architectural determinism suggests buildings have a direct and causal link to behavior. This position, however, does not do justice to the complexities of the environment, the complexities of behavior, nor the diversity of the students. It fails to capture the transactional relationship between buildings, students, and behavior; that is, it fails to sort out the complex social and psychological factors associated with built spaces (Porteus, 1977).

To view the relationship in terms of possibilities and probabilities, however, not only appears more realistic, it also captures our intuitive notion that campus buildings can make a difference in the lives of students.

What are the important behaviors that can be influenced by the architecture of the building? Deasy and Lasswell (1985), an architect and sociologist, respectively, outline eight behavioral categories that can be influenced by architecture. These categories have direct application to the campus environment. Deasy and Lasswell list these as follows: (1) friendship formation, (2) group membership, (3) personal space, (4) personal status, (5) territoriality, (6) communications, (7) cue searching, and (8) personal safety.

In other words, the architecture can make possible and increase probability of friendship and group involvement by designing spaces that bring people together. Personal needs of privacy and personalization can also be impacted by the architecture. Students, like all of us, seek private and personal spaces they can retreat to and call their own. Some spaces facilitate communication among students, and other space arrangements often hinder important communications. Classrooms can often be seen from this framework. Cue-searching or way-finding is the notion that the architecture can help us navigate the campus. The architecture can either confuse us or guide us. Finally, architecture of "doors" can either increase or decrease the probability of being safe.

Given the influence that architecture has on important student behaviors, Deasy and Lasswell's suggestion that all building/program plans of new construction or renovations should carry what they call "behavioral program" makes for good student affairs practice. Seeking out all messages related to campus material culture is likewise good student affairs practice.

Campus behavioral programs related to architecture and other elements of the material culture need not be a mystery. These behaviors can be detected by keen observation using nonverbal cues for the assessment or appraisal of the material artifacts.

This observational process can be used to gather information to assist in the diagnostic efforts as well as the selection of possible intervention strategies regarding organizational issues, such as campus diversity. What, then, are the conceptual tools that can lead to greater understanding of organizations and campus environments through the examination of the material culture?

### Physical Traces: A Conceptual Tool for Understanding the Organization

It is important to note that buildings and organizations have important direct functional relationships. For example, is there enough space to carry out the functions of the organization? The physical environment not only affords certain activities and constrains others in a functional sense (Wohlwill, & Heft, 1989), but these functional arrangements of affordances and constraints also communicate non-verbal messages (Weinstein & David, 1987). How can we increase our understanding of organizations by attending to the non-verbal messages of the organization's physical environment (Rapoport, 1982)? One of the more useful strategies is to view the organization's physical environment from a behavioral traces perspective (Zeisel, 1981), including the symbolic messages accompanying the behavioral trace (Rapoport, 1982; Steele, 1973).

As organizational activities interact with physical spaces, the behavior leaves "traces" (Bechtel & Zeisel, 1987). These behavioral traces can be interpreted as non-verbal messages that increase the understanding of campus behavior (Banning, 1988). As Bechtel and Zeisel state: "Few give a thought … to the fact that the fossils of tomorrow are the garbage dumps of today" (1987, p. 32). Zeisel (1981) presents a number of ways "to read" traces that can be useful in gaining a fuller understanding of organizational environments. Zeisel's methods are: (1) by-products of use, (2) adaptation of use, (3) displays of self, and (4) public messages.

## By-products of Use

*Photo A1 Erosion*

*Photo A2 Eroded Chair Arms*

By-products are produced by people interacting with the environment. These by-products of behavior can be further defined by the concepts of erosion, leftovers, missing traces, and accretions (Bechtel and Zeisel, 1987). A simple example of *erosion* on campus is the worn paths (shown in Photo A1) that students make as they find the shortest distance between campus buildings. Worn furniture in an admissions office waiting area is another example of erosion that has greater negative impact on institutional image. Worn or eroded armchairs suggest fiddling or nervousness (Photo A2). These are not the physical traces that suggest a comfortable admissions office visit.

*Leftovers* are traces represented by objects not consumed in the behavior. Trash and litter are the most common examples. Leftovers can also become associated with campus issues. For example, Photo A3 illustrates that students are unwilling to place recyclable items in a trash receptacle, and these leftovers are accumulating at the top. The issue could be resolved by adding a recycle bin for plastics. Another

*Photo A3 Trash Receptacle*

*Photo A4 Restroom*

example of leftovers can be found in Photo A4: Restroom. As a part of a task to view residence halls' material culture in relation to their mission statement (Banning & McKelfresh, 1998), the restroom photo was taken to illustrate the need to be more diligent and timely in the cleaning of restrooms. This restroom was designated for visitors to the residence hall, and the leftovers do not send a very positive public message.

Bechtel and Zeisel (1987) use the concept of *missing traces* to indicate a lack of use in areas where erosion and leftovers are expected but do not show up. Many campus spaces have been designed in such a manner as to ensure that they will never be used by people on campus. The documentation of this lack of use or "missing traces" is often helpful in gaining

*Photo A5 Bike Rack*

support for a redesign of the space to better serve the needs of the campus. For example, Photo A5 shows a bike rack unused despite heavy bicycle traffic on campus due to its location (not being near an entrance to the building). For better use, the bike rack needs to be moved closer to an entrance. Finally, the concept of *accretion* is used to denote the buildup of materials on physical objects. For example, dust on books in the library that have not been checked out or buildup of fingerprints on frequently used doorknobs.

**Adaptation for Use**

Zeisel (1981) uses the concept of adaptation for use to encompass situations in the environment where a change has been made because the first design did not serve its original intention. The physical environment is changed to better accommodate campus behavior. These adaptations or accommodations are classified by Zeisel (1981) as props, separations, and connections.

Campus adaptation for use would include renovations, expansions, and other changes or improvements. Often the attempt by students to "adapt" a space for an unintended purpose is the first cue that a redesign effort may be needed. Props are items that are added to or moved from a setting. For example, chairs (props) are often moved around in a building by students to better accommodate their seating patterns. By following the adding, moving, and removing of props from a setting, insights can be gained regarding inhabitant behavior. Photo A6 suggests that sitting for traditional telephone behavior is more desirable than standing.

*Separations* are those changes in which the inhabitants of the physical space separate spaces formerly together to achieve some

*Photo A6 Telephone Seat*

*Photo A7 Roomate Seperation*

behavioral outcomes. The creativity displayed by students in developing separations in the traditional residence hall room to achieve privacy and a sense of territory is a clear example.

*Connections* are physical adaptations that connect settings allowing for different behaviors. On one campus, a makeshift sidewalk appeared in order to connect the rear parking lot to the main entrance to a new student center. The need for this connection was due to the failure of the original design to place a rear entrance to the building. Physical connections can also produce symbolic connections. On one campus, a bridge was built to link two parts of a campus that had been separated by an irrigation ditch. The bridge, however, took on symbolic meaning when it was constructed in part from the bricks off "old main" that burned down during a Vietnam-era protest. The bridge was designed by a group of veterans as well as a group of protesters to the war and dedicated to bridge or "connect" the differing points of view toward the war.

### Displays of Self

Zeisel (1981) uses the concept of "display of self" to illustrate how the material cultural can be used to convey messages about individual and group ownership. Three categories represent this concept:

*Personalization* or the use of the physical environment to express uniqueness and individuality. Resident doors with adornments within a residence hall is an example.

*Photo A8 Oil Derrick*

*Identification* or the use of the physical environment to enable others to identify the function of the environment. For example, on one campus there is a small "oil derrick" atop the petroleum engineering building (Photo A8).

*Group membership* or the use the physical environment to

*Photo A9 Fraternity House*

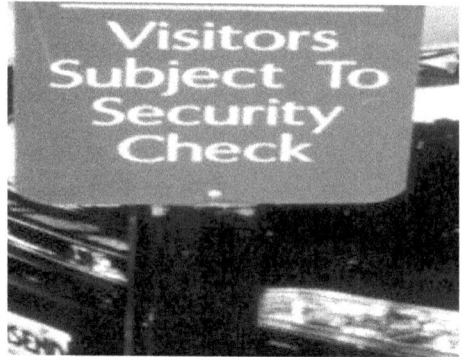

*Photo A10 Welcome Sign*

display membership in formal groups and organizations. The Greek letters on fraternity and sorority houses are a clear example. The "letter" display can also send non-verbal messages about organizational values. Fraternity houses that display artifacts of their activities send a clear message regarding house values. For example, the fraternity house in Photo 9A shows a disrespect for the American flag, a flying of the Confederate flag, and a "borrowed" Taco Bell advertisement banner.

**Public Messages**

The last category for Zeisel is public messages. Included in this concept are traces that range from official signs, unofficial signs and symbols, and graffiti. *Official signs* are erected by officials of the environment or organization. Often, however, these signs contain non-intended messages. For example, a welcome sign to visitors that also includes a warning that they may be searched while on campus is less than welcoming (Photo A10). *Unofficial signs* and symbols are those that appear in the environment but without formal sanctioning. On a campus, these

*Photo A11 Lost Sign*

*Photo A12 Redundant Signs*

usually take the form of written signs that often give directions to a particular building or office (Photo A11). When

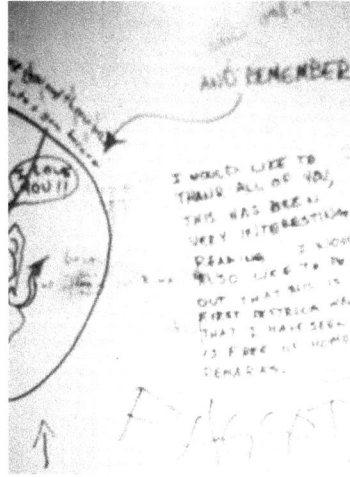

*Photo A13 Graffiti*

these signs begin to appear in multiple numbers (redundancy), it is usually an indication that the physical environment is not giving sufficient way-finding cues (Photo A12).

*Illegitimate* signs or messages often take the form of graffiti. Most observers of the campus environment are quite familiar with campus graffiti. It can signal creativity and local issues or give insight into prevailing attitudes on complex issues such as tolerance of diversity (Photo A13). In addition, the failure to remove illegitimate and offensive graffiti also sends messages regarding the institution's values.

## Summary

The concept of behavioral traces can be a useful tool for understanding organizations by observing the material culture. The environment is a medium of communication (Rapoport, 1982; Zeisel, 1975). Understanding this communication can assist in the campus appraisal and assessment process regarding campus issues, for example, diversity.

## References:

Banning, J. H. (1988). Behavioral traces: A concept for campus ecologist. *The Campus Ecologist, 7*(2), 1-2.

Banning, J. H., & McKelfresh, D. A. (1998). Using photographs of the housing mission Statementin staff training. *Talking Stick, 15*(8), 22-14.

Bechtel, R., & Zeisel, J. (1987). Observation: The world under a glass. In R. Bechtel, R. Marans, & W. Michelson (Eds.). *Methods in Environment and Behavioral Research* (pp. 11-40). New York: Van Nostrand Reinhold Company.

Bell, P., Fisher, J., Baum, A., & Greene, T. (1990). *Environmental psychology*. Fort Worth, TX: Holt, Rinehart and Winston, Inc.

Deasy, C. M. & Lasswell, T. (1985) *Designing places for people*. New York: Watson-Guptill Publications.

Porteus, J. (1977). *Environment and behavior*. Reading, MA: Addison-Wesley.

Rapoport, A. (1982). *The meaning of the built environment: A non-verbal communications approach*. Beverly Hills, CA: Sage Publications.

Steele, F. I. (1973). *Physical settings and organizational development*. Reading, MA: Addison-Wesley Publishing Company.

Weinstein, C., & David, T. (1987). *Spaces for children*. New York: Plenum Press.

Wohlwill, J., & Heft, H. (1989). The physical environment and the development of the child. In D. Stokols & I. Altman (Eds.), *Handbook of Environmental psychology, Vol. 1* (pp. 175-204). New York: John Wiley & Sons.

Zeisel, J. (1975). *Sociology and architectural design*. New York: Russell Sage Foundation.

Zeisel, J. (1981). *Inquiry by design*. Monterey, CA: Brooks/Cole.

# ABOUT THE AUTHOR

**James H. Banning**

Jim Banning is professor emeritus in the School of Education at Colorado State University. After receiving his Ph.D. in clinical psychology from the University of Colorado-Boulder, his career has focused on student services administration, ecological/environmental psychology, and the application of environmental psychology to educational settings. He has particularly focused on the application of the ecological perspective and the development of the campus ecology model and has taught a course in campus ecology in the Student Affairs in Higher Education Program at Colorado State University for more than thirty years and continues to teach an online version. In addition to teaching, Jim has had administrative leadership experience in the roles of Director of Counseling and Testing, University of Colorado; Vice Chancellor for Student Affairs, University of Missouri-Columbia; and Vice President for Student Affairs, Colorado State University. During his career, Jim has authored and co-authored several books, book chapters, and journal articles on the ecological perspective of student services, including the recent publications of *Designing for Learning: Creating Campus Environments for Student Success, Student Affairs Leadership: Defining the Role Through an Ecological Framework, Campus Ecology and University Affairs: History, Applications, and Future*; and *Organizations at the Intersections of Place.*

www.ingramcontent.com/pod-product-compliance
Lightning Source LLC
Chambersburg PA
CBHW060553100426
42742CB00013B/2539